The Ice Men

by Gary Ronberg

Special photography by Melchior DiGiacomo

A Rutledge Book
Crown Publishers, Inc.
New York, New York 10016

Fred R. Sammis	Publisher
John T. Sammis	Creative Director
Doris Townsend	Editor-in-Chief
Allan Mogel	Art Director
Jeanne McClow	Managing Editor
Jeremy Friedlander	Associate Editor
Gwen Evrard	Associate Art Director
Arthur Gubernick	Production Consultant
Penny Post	Production Manager
Margaret Riemer	Editorial Assistant
Sally Andrews	Editorial Assistant

Library of Congress Catalog Card Number: 72-82970
ISBN: 0-517-503751

Prepared and produced by Rutledge Books, Inc., 17 East 45th St.,
New York, N.Y. 10017

Published by Crown Publishers, Inc., 419 Park Avenue South, New
York, N.Y. 10016

Published simultaneously in Canada by General Publishing Company,
Ltd.

Published 1973

Printed in Italy by Mondadori, Verona

Contents

1

More Than a Game / 8

2

"Friday Is a Bum . . . Friday Is a Bum . . ." / 24

3

Pray That Orr Misses the Plane *by Punch Imlach / 60*

4 5 6 7

**The
Million-dollar
Power Play / 116**

**A
Private
Hell / 134**

**"Fighting
Is a Part
of the Game" / 170**

**Twelve Men:
A Consensus
Postwar,
All-Star Team / 202**

1 | More Than a Game

The emotions of hockey. *Above:* Begrudging congratulations for a new Stanley Cup champion. *Right:* Hadfield powers puck past Montreal's Dryden. *Opposite left:* Keith Magnuson is escorted off the ice following fight. *Opposite right:* Toronto and New York brawl and—a rare exception—the goalies join in.

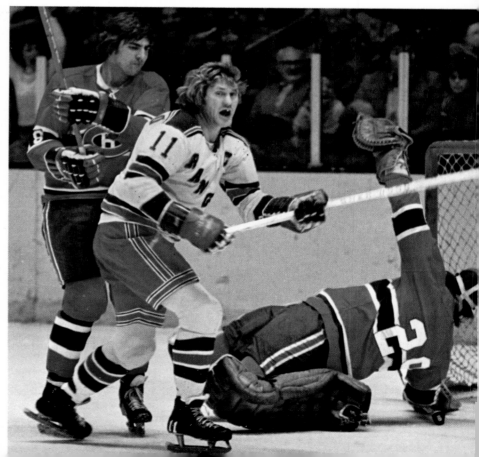

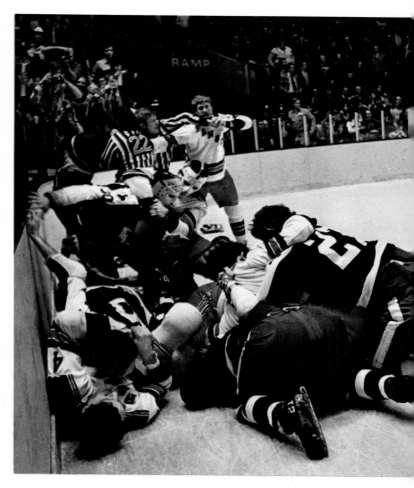

fusing, a game of luck. Also, there are moments, particularly when the teams are checking closely, when a game can be a cautious struggle at center ice. But then there is the puck behind the net, the center sweeping by and leaving it for the defenseman. A quick pass out to the right wing, who, challenged immediately, taps the puck off the boards, sidesteps the defender, then passes hard and true to the center, moving swiftly out of the zone.

An attack has burst into life. Opposing forwards, their forechecking efforts shredded by the razor-sharp passes, wheel in a desperate effort to catch up with the play. The defensemen turn and skate backward, facing them, challenging this threat.

The center feeds the puck to the left wing, breaking over the blue line into the attacking zone. The net covered, a defenseman bearing down upon him, the wing drops the puck back to the center, at the rim of the face-off circle. Now the right wing is cruising into the slot—25 feet out directly in front of the net. The center's pass is perfect. The shot imminent, the

wing's stick lifted in a high, wide arc, all action seems to freeze for an instant. . . .

Crack! Like a rifle shot, the puck shoots on a low, hard path to the goalie's left. Down he goes, his left leg kicking frantically. *Clank!* Hard rubber ricochets off the steel goalpost, and as the goalie scrambles back to his feet, players from both sides sweep past in pursuit of the puck, now loose in the corner. . . .

Hockey is two games unfolding at once. Which one a fan watches depends entirely upon where he sits. From high above the ice, the game is clearer, more comprehensible, than from ice level. A team's style, or lack of one, is apparent in cold, impersonal terms. Mistakes are left stark and immediately traceable, and a spectator in the balcony is apt to bluntly criticize the offender. At the same time, he is just as likely to observe a succession of smoothly interlocking passes and think, "A pretty play. A pretty play indeed." The detached, theater critic's view is possible because distance from the ice slows the game to a pace at which events can be anticipated.

I will never forget the sharp sense of impending doom I felt for the Boston Bruins at about 12:15 A.M. on May 8, 1969. The scene was a sweltering Boston Garden and, down 3–2 in games in their semifinal series against the Montreal Canadiens, the Bruins had thrown everything but the whirlpool bath at Montreal goalie Rogatien Vachon. Through three regular periods and well into double overtime, the stocky, sideburned goaltender had kicked out all that Orr, Esposito & Co. could throw at him. Time and again the Bruins had swept into the Montreal zone, firing on Vachon from all angles. Any second, through almost 30 minutes of stirring sudden-death overtime, *Les Canadiens* could have died with a bolt of red light from behind Vachon's net.

Then, about eight minutes into the second overtime, Boston defenseman Don Awrey directed a seemingly routine pass to wing Ron Murphy, starting up the left side just inside his blue line. I was sitting in a makeshift press box high in the corner farthest from the play, but to this day I can still see the blue number 14 of Claude Provost—"Little Joe"—stepping alertly inside Murphy and intercepting that pass. Perhaps 30 feet to the left of Provost loomed the mighty Jean Beliveau, the aging hero who hadn't had what could be called a good series. It was like watching the end of a movie I had seen a hundred times.

"I gave Claude a little yell and he gave me the puck," Beliveau said later. "I saw a lot of net over the [goalie's] left shoulder. It was a wrist shot. Twenty feet. I shot and hoped."

Bruin defenseman Ted Green slid skates-first in a desperate attempt to block the shot. Goalie Gerry Cheevers' left arm snapped upward—too late. "As soon as the puck hit Beliveau's stick it was gone," Cheevers would say. "By the time I got organized it was over my shoulder and in the net."

The red light flashed, and Beliveau wheeled away, his arms raised in victory. Green rolled over, saw the light and shook his head in disgust. Fellow defenseman Awrey sprawled face down in front of the net and covered his head with his arms. Cheevers flung his stick against the boards, and another Bruin, Ken Hodge, grasping his stick in both hands, cracked it over the crossbar.

So vivid, so neat, that play lives in my memory. Not because it meant the Stanley Cup for the Canadiens (who went on to defeat the St. Louis Blues in four straight games) but for its utter finality. That, and because I saw it coming.

The closer a spectator is to the ice, the more aware he is of the fury and human drama of a hockey game. At ice level, with his face almost pressed against the glass, he no longer sees a game of neatly positioned, conveniently numbered player-objects. Hockey becomes an explosive blur of color—reds and blues, greens and yellows, blacks and golds. The vibrant, frenzied action is ruthless and punishing. Suddenly hockey is near boards, far boards, our end, their end, the play sweeping upon us, in front of us, away from us in a flow of sound and activity.

The ice-level spectator is amid a world of real people—familiar people, whose faces he has seen countless times in newspapers and magazines and on television. Elevated several inches by their skates, hulking with their protective equipment, the heroes become human beings who run out of breath, scowl, grin, glisten with sweat in the glare of the lights. They shout, swear, thump down on the bench and run a towel through their hair. They ask for the water bottle and look up soulfully at the clock.

Down at ice level in Boston Garden that night, fans heard Beliveau's "*Claude!*" They saw the puck fly on a fast, rising plane, the burst of red light, Green's grimace, Cheevers's stick thudding against the boards, Hodge's splintering stick.

As the legs go, experience takes over. Harry Howell (opposite), at 40, helps captain and steady the Los Angeles Kings. Ron Harris, 16 (below), later to be traded, checks Vic Hadfield.

Hockey's growing popularity in the United States is due to more than its natural pulse and excitement. First, it is an easy game to understand; once exposed to hockey, one can be "expert" before the season is over. Second, the occasional blood-letting satisfies any fan's secret longing for violence. Last, and perhaps most important as far as Americans are concerned, hockey players have recently become more colorful and outspoken. They have become personalities.

Bobby Hull, hockey's goodwill ambassador of the sixties, would make the team bus wait until he signed every autograph. A superstar chafing under Chicago Black Hawk management, he finally joined the World Hockey Association for $2.5 million. Mod, immodest, brash, irreverent Derek Sanderson, hockey's Joe Namath, would climb into the stands to fight taunting fans. He jumped the champion Boston Bruins for a WHA offer of $2.65 million. Ken Dryden of Montreal, hulking, articulate, is in the winter the game's finest goaltender, in the summer, a horn-rimmed lawyer with "Nader's Raiders." Chicago's Keith Magnuson, red-haired, fiery, dead game, took karate lessons before his rookie year, then fought everyone in sight. Garry Unger, blond, longhaired, dated Miss America as a

Detroit Red Wing. Now traded, he rides motorcycles, wears cowboy boots and raises quarter horses on the owner's farm outside St. Louis. And, of course, Bobby Orr, who will never be called outspoken, performs feats on the ice that leave everyone speechless.

Before most of these players arrived, big-league hockey consisted of 6 tight, closemouthed clubs and 120 tight, closemouthed players. Competition for jobs was so fierce that two or three bad nights meant you were gone. Players like Red Berenson, Bill Goldsworthy, Cesare Maniago and Bill White either rode the bench or played in the minors. But the finished product was of the highest quality. There was no need to sell or promote hockey; hockey sold itself. When the Black Hawks began drawing solidly in the late fifties, the entire National Hockey League was playing to packed houses.

This was hockey that Canada worshiped. Her hockey heroes were national figures during their careers and instant legends when they retired. The sight of Maurice ("Rocket") Richard bearing down on a goaltender, defenders draped across his back, lives on in the taverns of Montreal. Many still believe he was the greatest goal-scorer of them all. The Rocket, they say, could find a loose puck in a pile of

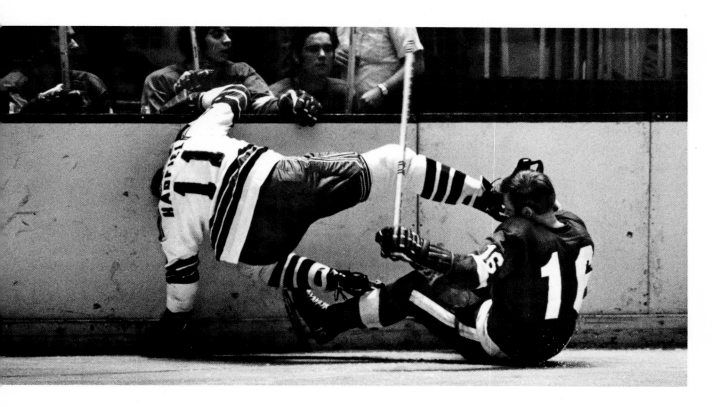

15

coal at midnight. Then there was Gordie Howe, Detroit's "Big Engine," who overcame a head injury that almost killed him and became the best all-around player in the game. And Jean Beliveau, tall, quiet, *Les Gros Bil* ("The Big Bull") of the Canadiens. Big Jean spoke with deeds, not words.

Charles Conacher, Dit Clapper. Eddie Shore, the most hated player of his time, the bald Bruin, who bashed heads with his fists and slashed them with his stick. Milt Schmidt, King Clancy. Howie Morenz of Montreal, *l'homme-éclair* (" top man") of the twenties, who changed his suits and spats three times a day, who skated so fast that all the others looked as though they were going backward, who broke four bones in his leg and ankle during a game in 1937 and died five weeks later, at 37, following an embolism.

Bernie ("Boom Boom") Geoffrion, Terry Sawchuck, Bobby Hull, Ted Lindsay, Jacques ("Jake the Snake") Plante . . . the list of greats is long and so are their records, records that, unfortunately, have been belittled by expansion.

There was a time not very long ago when scoring 20 goals in the National Hockey League was roughly equivalent to hitting .300 in baseball. A very good year, as the song goes. In a single year 30 goals was exceptional, 40, superior, and 50 goals—well, until Bobby Hull, only two players (Richard and Geoffrion) had ever scored 50 in a single season. When Hull got his 51st goal, in March of 1966, many compared it to Roger Maris breaking Babe Ruth's record of 60 home runs in a season. After all, even Howe had never scored 50 goals, nor had Beliveau or Frank Mahovlich.

But expansion brought inexpert backcheckers, defensemen and goalies. In 1970–71, Phil Esposito of the Bruins scored 76 goals. The next year he got 66. In 1971–72, a young left wing with the Buffalo Sabres, Rick Martin, scored 44 goals in his first playing year in the NHL.

Players like Milt Schmidt and Bob Pulford never had a 30-goal year. "The Pocket Rocket," Henri Richard, did it only once. In 14 years with Toronto and Montreal, Bert Olmstead got 20 goals only once. But in 1970–71, while Esposito was filling the net, John Bucyk got 50, 3 players scored 40, 15 had 30 and 46 got 20 goals!

The records for total points fell just as quickly. In the first 50 years of the NHL, nobody had scored 100 points in a season. Hull and Stan Mikita had each reached 97, Dickie Moore of Montreal, 96, and Howe

and Geoffrion, 95. But since the first year of expansion, NHL players have passed 100 points a dozen times, Esposito having scored the most in a season, 152.

According to the bromide, records are made to be broken. But the near obliteration of records that recorded the feats of hockey's greatest players has left Canadians and old-line fans in America bewildered and bitter. Expansion was inevitable, of course. With every other major sport loosening its belt, hockey had no choice but to do the same. The old fan understands that, but he cannot understand continued expansion when the breach between most of the old clubs and the new clubs is greater than ever before.

Every expansion reduces the appearances a team makes in an established league city. In 1965, for example, the Detroit Red Wings played seven games a year in Montreal, and the Habs played seven in Detroit. Often these games were part of home-and-home series, Saturday night—Sunday night affairs in which the emotions of one game inevitably extended to the next. Now, the Red Wings and Canadiens meet only four times all year (twice in each city), and their once-fierce rivalry is but a memory. The growing pains are evident elsewhere. "The only thing harder than getting tickets to Boston-Montreal," says one observer, "is giving away tickets to Oakland-Montreal."

The World Hockey Association is a story in itself. It is still hard to believe that the "Golden Jet," Bobby Hull, is now playing left wing in obscure, half-filled rinks across North America. Hull probably spoke for many an older player when, a few months before going to the WHA, he remarked, "Expansion diluted

"It was a national disaster when Team Canada lost two and tied one of its first four games against the Russians." But Brad Park *(opposite),* among others, led the Canadians to final victory. *Above:* Ranger coach Emile Francis takes to the ice to make a point.

the old pride that gave such prestige to playing in a six-team, one-hundred-twenty-man league. I'm afraid that pride may never be regained."

In spite of what the NHL and the WHA have done to hockey in recent years, Canada will stick by her game. It was never more evident than in the summer of 1972, when the whole country—including the Prime Minister—was in an uproar over Hull being left off the All-Star team that was to play the Russians in the fall. (The NHL's agreement with the USSR self-servingly provided that only players with signed NHL contracts were eligible for the series. Since Hull had signed with the WHA, he was ineligible.) When Prime Minister Trudeau urged that Hull be allowed to join the team, NHL president Clarence Campbell tried to explain. Trudeau flatly refused to see him.

Phil Esposito dared to hint he might not be able to play in the series because of contractual obligations to his hockey school in Sault Ste. Marie. Within hours after the news flashed across the country, the Boston star was swamped with telegrams and telephone calls branding him "unpatriotic" and "money hungry." Esposito played against the Russians, as he had wanted to all along. One feels that had he done anything else, he might never have had another Canadian boy in his hockey school.

Canada shows her allegiance to hockey in many ways. It was a national disaster in September of 1972 when Team Canada lost two and tied one of its first four games against the Russians, and a national celebration when the Canadians won three of the four games in Moscow, thereby winning the overall series.

And note the excellent condition of the major-league arenas in Montreal, Toronto and Vancouver. All three are immaculate and done in excellent taste. The Forum, recently remodeled for $9 million, has a stunning interior of red, white and blue. Maple Leaf Gardens has a softer blend, in blue, gray and white. The new Pacific Coliseum in Vancouver lacks only tradition. Hockey and Canada go hand-in-hand, and Canadians are proud of it; their top-rated television program is "Hockey Night in Canada." Nor was it accidental that the squad that represented them against Russia was named "Team Canada."

Canada's young are introduced to skates at age three, stitches at ten and dentures at fifteen. For decades, the dream of practically every boy in Canada has been to step onto the ice wearing the maple leaf of Toronto or the CH of Montreal on his breast. By the time he fails, and most do, hockey isn't

a game anymore. It's almost as sacred as God and family. It still warms him with anticipation and excitement when, as a man and a father, he takes the hand of his son and walks briskly through the cold wind to the arena and two much-valued seats in the balcony.

I will always remember the first National Hockey League game I saw. It was a game between the Red Wings and the Canadiens in Detroit, on a Sunday night in February of 1961—not a particularly important game, but I can't forget the sights, the sounds, the smells. There was a special feel to the game. I have a similar feeling at every hockey game I see. No other sport affects me like hockey.

As a journalism student at Michigan State University who was more than casually interested in sports, I had been assigned by the school newspaper to cover the college hockey team. It soon became apparent that a crash course in hockey was in order for me. A number of the players on the team were particularly helpful. When one of them, a French Canadian from Montreal, noticed that the Canadiens were coming to town, he said, "Ah yes, Garee. It is time you see the pros, how they do it. It is time we go see *Les Canadiens.*"

For someone who had grown up in Indiana, with a baseball field on one block and a basketball court

on another, it was a difficult invitation to refuse. Montreal was a faraway place with strange-sounding names: Ri-*chard,* Be-li-*veau,* Geof-fri-*on,* Jacques *Plante.* . . . And, of course, here was an opportunity to see this fellow Howe, about whom I had heard so many wonderful things.

Throughout the 90-mile drive to Detroit, I remember great concern over getting tickets. The Red Wings and Canadiens were furious rivals, I was told, and the game would be a sellout for sure. We had left early in the afternoon, two fraternity brothers of mine having assured us that if we arrived before the $1.50 balcony seats went on sale at 5:30, we would get in. We did.

I can still see Olympia Stadium as it awaited the

Hockey is many things. It's Phil Esposito being taken out of the play against Russia, Bruce Hood signaling for a face-off, Esposito and John Bucyk beginning a cheer for the team while Gary Bergman kneels dejectedly or Vic Hadfield reflecting after a game.

teams and their warm-up. Far below us was the ice; cold, hard. Except for vivid red circles and dark blue lines the ice seemed hazy. At each end of the playing surface were the nets, snow white against the cream of the ice, and the goalposts, gleaming red. The surface was enclosed by white boards, scarred with black, and a high shield of unbreakable glass. That ice, I remember, looked so cool, so tranquil, especially amid the murmur of the gathering crowd.

Suddenly, the floor of the arena exploded with light, a dazzling white glare. All at once I was aware of a network of lamps, hundreds of them, it seemed, suspended in long rows from the roof high above us. These game lights had been turned on as the Canadiens filed from the dressing room and one by one stepped onto the ice.

Les Habitants. "The Flying Frenchmen." *Les Canadiens.* There they were, right below me, but my first impression was that they looked tired and stiff, as if they had just stepped off an all-night train. (They had.) Even their uniforms looked tired. Meant to be white trimmed with red, they looked gray and dull orange, as if they had gone to the cleaners too often. The first Hab to catch my eye was Geoffrion, number 5, rock-hard, swarthy, slick black hair, his sweater, unknown to the Boomer, hitched unbecomingly on a hip pad. And there was Beliveau, tall, square-shouldered, obviously bull-strong. Henri Richard, Marcel Bonin, Tom Johnson, Doug Harvey, Plante—they were out there, too. But for some reason—maybe it was just the uniforms—this didn't look like a team that had finished first the last three years and had won five Stanley Cups in a row.

Especially when the Red Wings came trooping through their runway in seemingly silken red uniforms, trimmed in white, that unique Motor City winged wheel on their chests. To me, only the New York Yankee pinstripes can match the Detroit Red Wing uniform for class. Norm Ullman, Vic Stasiuk, Alex Delvecchio, Terry Sawchuck, Marcel Pronovost, all were immediately below me, skating in a large circle. But the only one I saw was Gordie Howe, cruising leisurely on one leg, then the other, that big white "9" on his back. He handled his stick, I remember, with unbelievable ease, as if it were balsa wood. Howe's stick cradled the puck like a fragile egg until, with an undetectable snap of his wrists, it suddenly became a hard black line to the waiting stick of a teammate. I watched Howe throughout the shooting drill. Although he did not put the puck past Hank Bassen,

who would play goal this night, all of his shots seemed to be on the corners. High, low, waist-high—but always on a corner. Then the buzzer sounded, and each team skated in a large circle again, faster and harder this time, before returning to their dressing rooms while the ice was resurfaced.

This was a big one for Montreal. The Canadiens trailed first-place Toronto by only two points. If they won tonight, and the Leafs lost in New York, Montreal would tie for first. In fourth place, the Wings had a 12-point lead on fifth-place New York in the race for the final play-off spot, and they trailed third-place Chicago by six. It looked like the Wings would make the play-offs, which was the big thing to them, but for a Montreal club coached by Toe Blake to finish lower than first would be a disaster.

The game was less than four minutes old when Howie Young, the Red Wings' tempestuous defenseman, was sent off for high-sticking Ralph Backstrom. The Habs, no longer looking stiff and worn out but like the champions they were, rolled in on Bassen in waves. Twelve seconds before the penalty would have expired, Bill Hicke, at the side of the net, converted passes from Bonin and Richard for a 1–0 lead.

At 8:34, balding Gerry Odrowski of Detroit wound up from 55 feet away and beat Jacques Plante for, as we found out later, his first goal in 55 games. More than 14,000 people, many without seats, loved it. "Jake the Snake," as he was called for his roaming style, was a popular figure in the Olympia but for all the wrong reasons.

Less than a minute later, however, Geoffrion picked off a clearing pass and blasted his 38th goal to put the Canadiens back in front. It was a big goal, not only for the Habs but for the Boomer, who was dueling Toronto's Frank Mahovlich for his second straight scoring title. Seconds later, Geoffrion was caught in a violent pileup in front of the Detroit net and left the ice for the remainder of the period, blood streaming from a gash in his cheek.

The period ended with no further scoring. It had been a good one, I thought; lots of action, the Detroit coach (Sid Abel) raging at the call on Howie Young. And I had actually seen two of the three goals. But my Canadian connoisseurs, as well as those from Detroit, were less than impressed with the play. Very ragged, they explained. Bad goal on Plante, bad Detroit pass on the goal by Geoffrion. Put in my place, I decided to observe the second period skeptically.

My resolve lasted two and a half minutes into the

second period before I was jumping up and down again. So were thousands of others, for Gordie Howe had just taken Delvecchio's rebound, faked Plante here and put it up there, tying the game 2–2. It was an exhibition of simple strength and savvy under fire. With bodies tumbling and sticks slashing around him, Howe had waited until the cagey Plante made the first move. As I was to read in the papers the next morning, it was Gordie's 500th career goal and his 463rd in regular season competition.

I had been advised to keep an eye on Howe, not only to see how he scored and set up his teammates, but to see what happened to opponents who got too close to him. A quick elbow, a glove in the face, a stick he could use like a sword—nobody crowded Gordie Howe. Not many fought with him, either. But with the action of my first game swirling below me, I didn't notice Howe's finer points.

A few years later, I got the idea. The Canadiens were again playing in Detroit when rookie defenseman Terry Harper spotted Howe in the corner and apparently decided that the best way to build a reputation was to challenge the best. Into the corner he went, 6 feet 3, 195 pounds, crashing into Howe with a high stick and raised elbows. Surprisingly, Howe appeared oblivious to it all. There was no penalty. As the play moved away my attention went with it.

Then, from that corner, came a crash that seemed to shake the building. I looked back, and saw Howe skating away, blinking innocently, leaving Harper behind in a crumpled heap. Although the rookie managed to pick himself up and skate back to the bench, he quietly missed his next few turns on the ice.

In that first game, the score was still tied halfway through the second period when Beliveau tipped Geoffrion's blast over Bassen's shoulder to put the Canadiens ahead, 3–2. The period finished that way, though the Wings outshot Montreal 16 to 7. Through a stirring third period, Montreal tried to ice the contest with another goal, Detroit fought desperately to tie. But the furious pace only set the stage for the finish.

With 1:31 left, J. C. Tremblay of the Canadiens was banished for holding Delvecchio. With 56 seconds to go and a face-off in the Montreal zone to the left of Plante, Abel pulled Bassen. The crowd tensed as the teams lined up, Howe and Delvecchio stationed at the points, Ullman facing off against Donnie Marshall. The puck was dropped, and Ullman fired it

against the boards to the left of Plante. Leo Labine, a right wing just acquired from Boston, raced in and without looking backhanded the puck to the blue line. The errant pass shot between the point men, into the neutral zone and straight toward the open net. Startled, Howe and Delvecchio wheeled and struck out in pursuit, churning away from us, heads down, elbows pumping. Over the blue line the puck went, slower now, Howe and Delvecchio gaining but not enough. As the puck slid into the open goal, dead center, the two Red Wings peeled away, Howe whacking his stick on the ice in anger. I was stunned. Almost 15,000 others buzzed in disbelief. Leo Labine had just scored one of the longest goals in National Hockey League history, shooting the puck 200 feet into his own net.

I left my first hockey game knowing I would return again and again. To me, as for so many others, hockey would always be more than another hot item.

More, even, than a game.

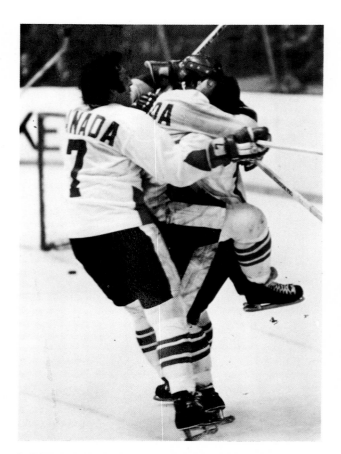

Phil Esposito and teammate bear-hug Paul Henderson, who became a household name in Canada when, in the waning minutes, he scored the winning goal to defeat USSR.

2 | "Friday Is a Bum... Friday Is a Bum"

It's not just Bill Friday. It's any man who ever put on a black-and-white shirt and skated onto the ice in any NHL city. To the fans, the referee is a bum, a crook, a chicken, a rat, a dog, a slob or a gutless coward. In truth, a referee in the National Hockey League is a superior kind of man.

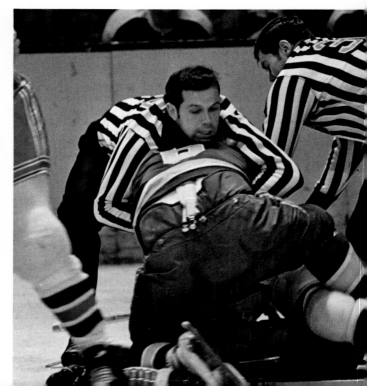

A referee or linesman is always in the middle.
"Your image is important," says Bruce Hood, at left
(top). "You have to project a sense of confidence."

but this is hardly sticking out one's neck when each team is likely to score 100 points or more. And in football, the longest possible penalty is 15 yards on a 100-yard field. Only in hockey does a routine penalty force one side to carry on shorthanded for the next two minutes.

Can you imagine a football team playing without its quarterback for two minutes of offense . . . or a baseball team without its shortstop for two outs? Only in hockey is the extra man as much a part of the game as the puck, and whenever that extra man helps put the puck in the net—as he often does—the referee had better be ready to defend that penalty against anyone from gallery gods to viewers of instant replay.

So why does anyone in his right mind aspire to be a referee in the National Hockey League? The truth is, few do. Most of today's referees got into officiating only when it became apparent they had no future as players or when they saw a chance to have some fun and make a few extra bucks in a local amateur league. John Ashley, the dean of the NHL officiating staff before he retired in 1972, says he became a referee because it seemed a logical step after years of playing in the minors. Wally Harris, who spent years refereeing amateur games around Montreal and in upstate New York, remembers that "it sounded like fun" when he was offered a crack at the "glamour" and "travel" of the big league. ("Of course, at the time I had no idea how much adventure was involved," he says now, laughing.) And Bruce Hood, confessing to the boyhood dream of growing up to be a cop, says, "Maybe I'm subconsciously directing traffic out there."

"Why did I become a referee?" asks Bill Friday, almost as if he never stopped to think about it. "Because I'm a different breed of cat, that's why. We all are. Like, would *you* put up with what we put up with?"

One thing is certain: No one goes into it for money. True, expansion has upgraded the salary of the NHL referee to about $20,000 a year—and as much as $27,000 if he is selected to work the play-offs—and has aided him in landing an improved pension plan. But one is almost tempted to compare any such security to the combat flight pay of a jet pilot: Is it worth the flak?

"I remember when I broke in back in 1960," says Friday. "I made thirty-four hundred dollars for the regular season and five thousand dollars including play-offs. We had four children at the time and, believe me, it took some odd jobs during the summer to make ends meet."

Hood and Harris both recall having to think long and hard before signing with the NHL; each was making more in another job than what the league offered (about $4,500). Also, advancement was not guaranteed and several years of minor-league seasoning were in prospect before a referee ever saw a National Hockey League arena.

"I'll never forget my first trip as a professional referee," says Hood. "It was to Memphis, and I arrived the day before the game. I checked into the hotel, went up to my room and started to unpack. Then I looked around. There was a bed, a night table and a desk, and the only light was a bulb hanging from the ceiling. No TV. No radio. The walls were something drab, gray or tan. And I didn't know anybody in Memphis.

"I sat down on that bed and thought, 'I gave up a good job for *this?*'"

"My wife remembers my first few months as a referee better than I do," says Harris. "I was gone for thirty-four days, home for two, then gone for thirty-six more."

Once he makes the NHL, a referee's travel schedule improves considerably, but it will never again be as it was prior to expansion, when the longest trip was between Chicago and Boston. Now, with the league reaching to the West Coast and as far south as Atlanta, a referee handling four games a week is constantly on the go. Take Bill Friday. When with the NHL, he might leave his home in Hamilton, Ontario, on Monday and drive to Buffalo, 60 miles away, to catch a plane for a Tuesday night game in Boston. On Wednesday he would go to Philadelphia for Thursday night, then on to Pittsburgh for Saturday night. Following a game in Chicago Sunday night, he would return home for a few days before a similar ritual began again. Trips to the West Coast are more hectic —and so are those schedules followed by NHL linesmen. A two-week stretch for veteran Neil Armstrong, for example, went as follows:

Tuesday, March 14—leave home (Sarnia, Ontario) for Chicago
Wednesday, March 15—at Chicago
Thursday, March 16—at Minnesota
Friday, March 17—travel to Los Angeles
Saturday, March 18—at Los Angeles
Sunday, March 19—at Oakland
Monday, March 20—travel to Minnesota

Tuesday, March 21—at Minnesota
Wednesday, March 22—at St. Louis
Thursday, March 23—return home
Friday, March 24—leave for Montreal
Saturday, March 25—at Montreal
Sunday, March 26—at Boston
Monday, March 27—return home
Tuesday, March 28—off
Wednesday, March 29—leave for Toronto

There was one pre-expansion trip, Armstrong recalls, in which he did not sleep in a stationary bed for five nights. "After a game in Toronto on Wednesday night, I took a train to Montreal for Thursday," he said. "After that game it was an overnight sleeper back to Sarnia, and on Friday night a midnight train to Chicago. After the game in Chicago it was a train to Detroit and, after that one, a train back to Chicago. By that time I was beginning to wonder if I'd be able to fall asleep in a bed that *wasn't* moving."

Armstrong also says that in 15 years as a linesman, he has not spent a Christmas Day when he was not arriving, leaving or working a game that night. "My family likes to eat," he says dryly. "But seriously, a traveling salesman works something like fifty weeks a year and he's gone five days out of seven. Me, I'm gone five or six days a week, but then I've got the whole summer off. [Armstrong is a golf pro at a local course from late spring to early fall.]

"It sounds like a lot of travel, and it is. But you won't hear me complaining. I enjoy the work."

The NHL requires that referees and linesmen travel independently of teams at all times. If, however, there is only one flight to a particular city, the officials upgrade to first class.

With the NHL now spreading across North America like spilled ink—and also responsible for supplying officials for the Western, Central and American Leagues—referees have never been in greater demand. Soon after expansion, the point was reached at which the NHL could no longer wait for potential officials to develop in the Canadian amateur leagues; suddenly almost anyone who showed a hint of promise was assigned to on-the-job training in the minors. How acute the situation has become is evident in the fact that in 1965 the NHL's entire complement of referees and linesmen totaled 19. Now, seven years after expansion, the number has swelled to 42.

Many observers are convinced that, just as the quality of hockey has suffered through hasty expansion, so too has the quality of officials. Many referees

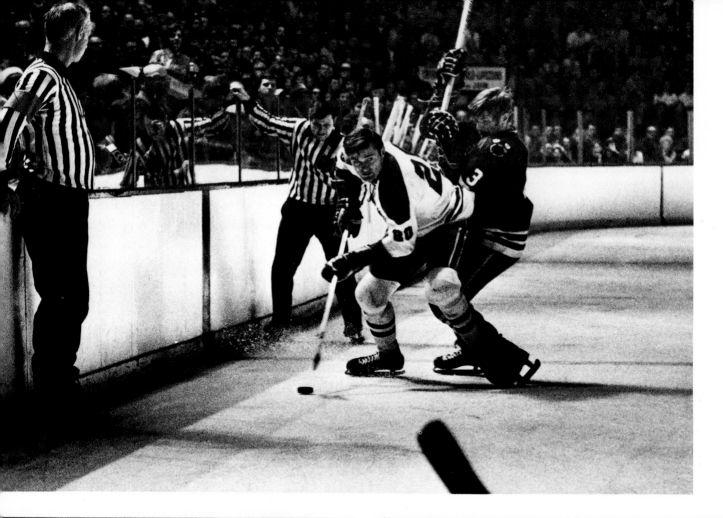

Bill Friday: "You can't call everything out there. If you did, there'd be no game because there's always something illegal going on." Judgment is the key, whether it's a case of high-sticking *(top)*, where to face-off *(left)* or cross-checking *(above)*.

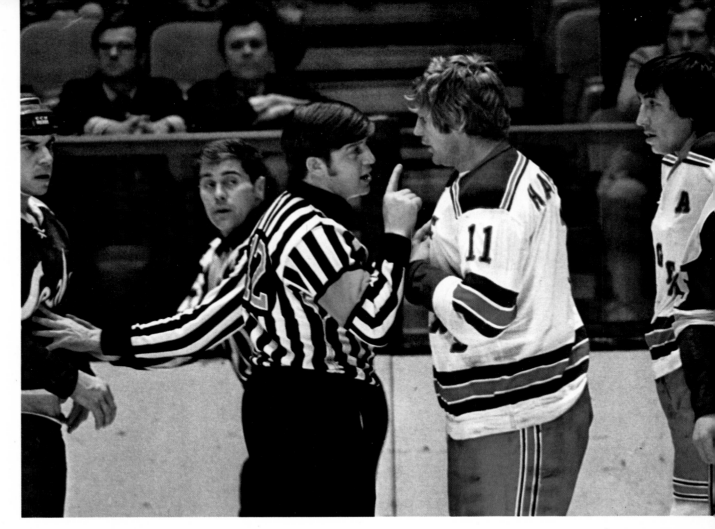

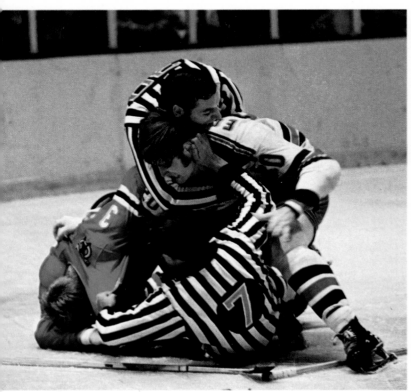

A referee must have iron in his soul, especially when breaking up a fight. The new, third-man rule has successfully cut down on large-scale brawls.

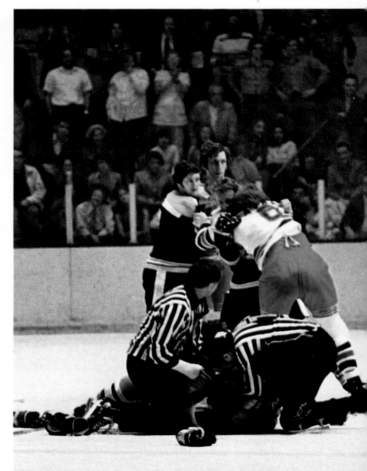

operate their own instructional schools in Canada, and the NHL itself has an intensive training program. But there is no substitute for experience, and some officials—Wally Harris for one—insist that the road is especially rough for anyone lacking a background in the amateur leagues.

"It may not sound like much, but stop to think about it," Harris says. "In the amateurs everything is simplified. It's player versus player, fan versus fan, town versus town. Everybody knows everybody else. There are no secrets. Rivalries are intense. It's not like the NHL, where the only time a fan sees a player is on the ice or on TV.

"Then, there are the rinks. In the amateurs they're nothing more than four walls with a tin roof on top to keep the wind out. There's no heat, so when it's twenty below outside, it feels like forty below inside because of the humidity. So the only way those fans can keep from freezing is by drinking that cheap Geneva gin. By the second period they're bombed, smashed out of their minds. Compared to fans like that, the crowds in Boston or New York or St. Louis are a piece of cake."

Harris says that the turning point in his career as a referee probably came in the amateur leagues, during the Montreal Junior B play-offs between Rosemont and Nationale in 1958.

"Here are two towns, situated side by side," says Harris. "Their teams share the same building all year long. It seats about seven thousand, so when both teams wind up in the finals, it's thirty-five hundred for one and thirty-five hundred for the other. Going into the fourth game, one team only leads the other by two games to one."

With only 12 seconds left in the game and the score tied, 2–2, Rosemont scores. One side of the rink erupts, the other falls silent. But Harris, parked to the side of the net, has spotted a Rosemont player in the crease, and without hesitation, he disallows the goal. Nationale rooters go berserk, while Rosemont cheers sour into boos. A half-hour is required to clear the ice for the remaining seconds of regulation time.

"The teams go into sudden death, and wouldn't you know it, Nationale scores to win, 3–2," says Harris. "Now the Rosemont fans are ready to lynch me. I beat it to the officials' room, lock the door and get ready for a long wait. It's an ugly mob outside that door, and I can hear them giving the police a helluva time. Those fans sound like they're trying to tear the rink down.

"It's two-thirty in the morning before I finally leave, and there are hundreds of Rosemont fans still waiting. But the police are there and—get this—*eight* squad cars escort me away from the rink. How many people ever get a police escort in their entire lives, let alone eight squad cars!"

By the next morning, feeling was running so high that the league suggested to Harris that perhaps someone else should handle the fifth game, which was two nights later. "I'm no hero," Harris says, "but I insisted upon handling that game. I'm pretty nervous when I skate onto the ice, but the crowd was really well behaved. A few boos and curses, of course, but nothing serious. As it turned out, the game was a snap. A laugher. No trouble at all.

"I've often thought back to that experience. I really think it had a lot to do with my becoming a referee in the NHL. And like I said, it took place in the amateurs, where anything not only can happen—it usually does."

Says Clarence Campbell, "These are very special men. They're like the old Spitfire pilots. Hard-fisted. Strong-willed. Bringing the plane in on the seat of their pants. They're instinctively capable of handling tight situations. A referee in the National Hockey League must have iron in his soul. Total, complete confidence in his instinctive judgement, without fear of the consequences. Such men are rare."

"Judgment is the most important ability you can have as a referee," says Bill Friday. "You can't call everything out there. If you did, there'd be no game because there's always something illegal going on. As a result, you've got to rely on your judgment—and hope that it's good."

A case in point, says Friday, is interference. "A minor penalty," states the NHL's 1972–73 rule book, "shall be imposed on a player who interferes with or impedes the progress of an opponent who is not in possession of the puck, or who deliberately knocks a stick out of an opponent's hand. . . . In calling interference, the referee should make sure which of the players is creating the interference, for often it is the attacking player which causes the interference, since the defending players are entitled to 'stand their ground' or 'shadow' the attacking players. . . ."

If interference was interpreted literally, or as it appears in the rule book, Friday says it would be called 30 to 40 times a game. "Just about every time one winger shadows another winger, he's interfering with him—if you interpret it literally," says Friday.

"Not to mention what goes on in front of the net, where the defensemen are trying to clear, and the forwards are trying for a shot or a rebound. Hockey is a rough game. By its very nature it's going to produce a lot of pushing and shoving. And interference."

"It seems like you're always looking at something you could call," says Wally Harris. "But that's where judgment comes in.

"There are times you wish you hadn't blown your whistle. But when you've done it, it's done. You've got to act like you couldn't be more certain of anything in your life. Never, ever hesitate. Hesitation is the first sign of indecision. And if the players think you're undecided, they'll sure as hell try and help you decide.

"All referees agree that second-guessing is out. A referee must trust his instinctive judgment, then act upon it; if he stops to make sure, he's finished. But the natural tendency to replay a tough game in one's mind and the internal turmoil that accompanies it is precisely the reason most referees dread being alone for extended periods of time."

Win, lose or tie, players enjoy a few beers together after a game. They share the satisfaction of having played well and, conversely, they boost each other's ego when they haven't played well.

"But where does the referee go?" asks Campbell. "Or more importantly, who does he go out with if his linesmen have to leave right after the game?

"Well, he'll probably go out by himself, that's what he'll do. And sometimes that can be like going out with his worst enemy. He made mistakes during the game. Of course he did. He's a human being. But, unable to talk to someone about those mistakes, he might start playing them over in his mind, building them out of proportion—second-guessing himself here, wishing he'd done something else there. That's when a referee can be heading for trouble, because it could affect his next game, the game after that, and so on for quite a while.

"After a particularly rough night, a referee just doesn't go back to his hotel and fall asleep. He collapses from physical and emotional exhaustion."

A perfect example of what Campbell is talking about is John D'Amico, a short, balding man with brown, soulful eyes and a quick smile, a referee who chose instead to return to working the lines.

"I was driving myself to the nut house," says D'Amico. "The day of a game I would lie on my bed, shaking like a leaf. Then psoriasis would break out all over my body. . . .

"I'd always dreamed about being a referee in the National Hockey League. When I was working my way up, I was on cloud nine. Me, an Italian construction worker who didn't get past grade ten, working the lines for four thousand dollars. Officials like to make it to the big leagues, just like the players do.

"But I'm a worrier. I worry about things I shouldn't. My goal is to do my job perfectly. That's impossible, of course, but I try anyway. When I was a ref, I was okay once I got on the ice. But I was a wreck all day, and as soon as the game ended I was worrying about the next one."

After refereeing 22 NHL games, D'Amico asked to be returned to the lines. His request was granted, with a $7,000 cut in salary.

"The guys thought I was crazy, going back to the lines. But I've got my health. And what's money anyway? Me and a millionaire, we both can eat off only one plate at a time. Besides, my wife said either the whistle goes or she goes."

"D'Amico was a good referee," says his boss, Scotty Morrison. "But he made the right decision. I remember when he was a referee, you'd shake his hand and it would be limp, like a fish. Now you shake it and his grip is firm, strong."

Rare is the referee who, at one time or another, has not fought similar battles with his nerves. Bruce Hood is another who almost quit before he went on to become one of the finest referees in the league.

"It was the roughest time of my life," Hood recalls. "I'd had a good year in 1967–68, the first year of expansion. It was the first year in which the majority of my games were in the NHL, and I was actually a bit surprised at how well it went. So I was confident going into 1968–69.

"But right from the start I began laboring. What had come so easily the year before all of a sudden seemed to require a great deal of effort. My confidence began to slip. By late December, I was fighting myself.

"In this business, January and February can be pretty depressing months. I was scheduled on the West Coast for some Western League games, and on the way out I had a couple of NHL games in which there was some minor controversy. One, I remember, was Chicago-Minnesota.

"After that my schedule was Portland at Phoenix for two games, then Portland at San Diego, Seattle and Vancouver—one game in each city. Well, the first night in Phoenix I had to disallow a Phoenix goal when the goal judge turned on the red light even

Rules are not meant to be taken literally, and unless an infraction is fairly obvious, the referee will not call it. Here, Bob Plager technically cross-checks Bruce MacGregor, but there's no penalty.

though the puck hadn't gone in the net. Everybody from Phoenix was down my back, and the crowd was mad as hell.

"The very next night I have to do the same thing, only this time it's against Portland. Their coach, Hal Laycoe, is so mad he leaves the bench and tries to get at the goal judge. His players are right behind him, and a riot almost breaks out. Players and fans were climbing the glass and everything. Two in a row! I couldn't believe it. I kept asking myself, 'Why me? Why me?'

"Next was another tough game in San Diego. Guys were swinging their sticks all over the place, and I had the penalty box jammed practically the whole game. I was really depressed by then, and when I got to Seattle, naturally it was raining. I checked into the hotel, went up to my room and never felt more alone. Or more miserable. Nothing can be worth this, I thought. Finally, I just decided to quit. I picked up the phone and called Scotty. He answered, and then for some reason I couldn't talk. He kept saying, 'Bruce . . . Bruce . . . what's the matter . . . ?'

"At last I was able to get it out. He said he was aware of the trip, aware that it had been a rough one. He asked me to work the game that night and then come home. I did, and the next day, when my wife picked me up at the airport, I broke down on the drive home.

"That was a Saturday. On Tuesday I had lunch with Scotty. I didn't know what I wanted to do. We talked for a long time and decided that I'd take the rest of the week off, then work the New York at Montreal game Saturday night.

"Well, those two clubs skate like hell. They always do, and it was a fine game. A good game for me. After it was over my two linesmen, Ron Ego and Bob Myers, took me to a great little bar in Montreal and got me so drunk I couldn't see. I know it was a great bar, but I was so smashed I can't remember where it was, and I haven't been back there since.

"As it turned out, the whole miserable experience was the best thing that could have happened to me. I learned that I'm my own worst critic, and I think I know how to handle it now. I take the good with the bad and try not to let the bad games get me down."

In 12 years as a National Hockey League referee, during which time he became number one on the staff, John Ashley officiated 680 games, including play-offs. And when three series during the 1971 play-offs reached seven games, Ashley handled the seventh game, each time before a roaring capacity crowd.

On the morning of the third game of the 1972 finals between the Bruins and the Rangers, Ashley sat in a coffee shop in midtown Manhattan and reflected on his job. Only a few people other than he knew that the game that night would be his last, that he would announce his retirement a month later.

"Why should I worry about tonight?" he said. "Everything that could possibly happen tonight has already happened to me somewhere along the line, so nothing will surprise me. When the final buzzer sounds, the game will be over. My job will be over. There's nothing I can change, even if I wanted to."

All referees have their distinctive qualities. Of the few who insist they don't grow unusually tense before a game, none insists more convincingly than John Ashley. Tall, bronzed and in his early forties, Ashley has the distinguished look of a bank president. Off the ice, fine clothes hang comfortably and naturally on his angular frame. The graying hair, worn in a short cut, completes the image. Ashley talks a good game, as most good executives do, using short, positive sentences which leave little room for disagreement. Perhaps as dean of the NHL officials, Ashley feels obligated to exude super confidence; whatever the reasons, he does it well.

"I'm a professional," Ashley maintains. "I do the very best I can. Time, I think, has proved that my best was more than good enough. Tonight's game is a big game. All play-off games are. But I've refereed so many games that tonight is really just another hockey game. When it's over I probably won't even know the score. I concentrate on my job, not the score."

That night, in 1972, Ashley refereed his last NHL game as he had refereed hundreds before it. Cruising along the boards with long, effortless strides, arms swinging at his sides, he was the model of detachment. Penalties were called in a calm, matter-of-fact manner, with no trace of emotion: John Ashley, banker, foreclosing on a bad debt.

Second period. New York led, 4–1. Madison Square Garden was constant bedlam, the capacity crowd roaring with every rush of the white-shirted Rangers. This was going to be the Rangers' game, the game that would draw them within one victory of tying the series. A win on Sunday *would* tie it, and after that . . . .

Stationed off to the side of the Boston goal, Ashley seemed unaware of the score or the crowd. The game was going well: hard-hitting but clean, a minimum of disputes. That's all that mattered to John Ashley.

Then Bobby Orr and Pete Stemkowski were wheeling and sweeping into the corner, elbow to elbow. In their path, a sapling before twin bulldozers, stood Ashley. There was no place for him to go. To the right, the speeding Orr . . . to the left, the charging Stemkowski . . . to the rear, the boards and the high glass—over which Ashley would soon be sailing.

John Ashley, professional referee, Blue Cross number . . . .

But then, like a bullfighter in his finest moment, Ashley turned sideways. Orr and Stemkowski flashed by, each thoughtfully tucking in an elbow, and continued their race for the puck. Disaster averted as quickly as it had developed, Ashley completed a 180-degree turn in time to whistle the play dead in the corner.

At the other end of the spectrum from Ashley is, of course, Bill Friday, a peacock strutting his stuff, a flamboyant, effervescent character whose stage is a white sheet of ice and his cue almost any stoppage in play. To Friday, a swarthy, thick-necked man with coal-black hair and pale-blue eyes, a referee's signals are not duties to be performed; each is a part to be enacted to the fullest.

Heated disputes bring out the best in Bill Friday. Skating slowly backwards, his head nodding emphatically, hands upraised in pacification of a disturbed old pro, the impression is graphic: "Damn it Alex, it didn't go in . . . the puck didn't go in the net . . . now Alex, take it easy . . . you know me better than that . . . do you *really* think I'd say it didn't go in the net if it did?"

When such a scene unfolded against the Rangers in New York, a now-famous chant always started somewhere in the balcony—before sweeping throughout Madison Square Garden. ". . . Friday is a bum . . . Friday Is A Bum . . . FRIDAY IS A BUM . . . !"

Says one fan in St. Louis, "For the longest time my wife couldn't stand Friday. Thought he was nothing but a big showboat, the way he carried on out there. Every time, he seemed to stir up the crowd. One night my wife was so upset she just had to talk to him. We waited for him to come out, and once he did, my wife went up and really told him off. Well, you know what Bill Friday did? He stood there for fifteen minutes, explaining every call she didn't like.

"Friday's a cool guy. He really is. I don't know what he told my wife that night, but now she thinks he's the greatest referee in the world."

Bill Friday believes a referee's job is something akin to being on stage. Even the act of dropping the puck for a face-off is an opportunity to emote.

Because he is an extrovert, thoroughly outgoing and friendly, Friday seems to converse with players more frequently than do his colleagues. However, since he is a fine referee—and both he and the players know it—Friday probably takes more ribbing than ripping. An example would be the afternoon Gordie Howe was sitting in the stands with Friday's children while the referee was instructing a hockey clinic.

"Say, how did you get down here?" Howe asked.

"Oh, Dad brought us down."

"No, I mean how did you *really* get down here?"

"Really, Gordie. Dad drove us down."

"Well, in that case I think the authorities should be notified."

"But Gordie . . . why?"

"Because your Dad can't see."

Most referees fall somewhere in between Ashley and Friday in style and composure. Tall and lithe, his jaw set, his mouth a thin, straight line, Bruce Hood has developed a quiet but forceful exterior. It is, he admits, something he must work at all the time.

"Your image is important," he says. "You have to project a sense of confidence. Of decisiveness. If you have a tendency to question yourself and it shows, crowds like those in St. Louis and New York and Boston will get you to wondering whether you really are right.

"So when you make a call, it's made. No matter how hot they make it for you, no matter what the pressure, you can't get ruffled or flustered. You're the one who's in command, and you've got to show it. You've got to realize that you're the only sane person in the building and all the rest are idiots."

Citing an example of a cool head and strong will under fire, Scotty Morrison refers to a game Hood handled between the Pittsburgh Penguins and the St. Louis Blues. "Pittsburgh is going into the St. Louis zone when a player is fouled. Hood signals a delayed penalty, and there's a scramble in front of the net. The goal judge puts the light on by mistake. The puck doesn't go into the net, and Fran Huck of St. Louis falls on the puck and pulls it under him. Whistle.

"Hood now has to make some vital calls in sequence. First, wash out the goal. Second, award a penalty shot to Pittsburgh, which is automatic for falling on the puck in the crease.

"As it happens, Pittsburgh does not score on the penalty shot, but Hood still has to call the original two-minute penalty he had delayed on. St. Louis ob-

jected strongly, but Hood had made the call just right."

"Players are the greatest con artists in the world," says Clarence Campbell. "They'll come on all sweetness and light, buddying up to you—then they'll carve you up so fast you won't know what happened."

"It's toughest when you're breaking in," explains Friday. "What you need is confidence, but there's nobody on that ice—or in the whole building, for that matter—who's going to help you get it. You're alone, and they'll always be testing you, asking if you're sure, chipping away, trying to break you. It can still get pretty hairy out there when you've got players from both sides down your back and eighteen thousand people trying to make up your mind for you. But it's nothing like when you're trying to break in."

"I'll never forget the first NHL game I ever had," says Hood. "It was an exhibition game between Chicago and Detroit at St. Catharines, Ontario, where the Hawks train. Naturally, I was pretty nervous. Glenn Hall was in goal for Chicago. I later found out he always talked a lot out there. But I didn't know it at the time, and when Detroit scored Glenn really let me have it. He argued that the Red Wings had a man in the crease. He was really hot, made me feel like a flea. When I skated over to the scorer's bench, I couldn't even feel my knees. I was that shook. If Glenn had said anything more right then, I wouldn't have been able to skate."

"Respect from players takes time," says Wally Harris. "A short time for a few refs, a long time for most. You just can't browbeat a player into respecting you. You can't say 'I'm the ref, I'm the boss.' You have to earn their respect. But if you're fair and consistent, and it's obvious to them that you're trying to be that way, they'll come to respect you. They'll make it rough, though. They'll always make it rough. They'll run you out of the league if you let them."

"After a while," says Friday, "you start to take it all in stride. The intimidation, the attempts at embarrassment—it becomes part of the job and you don't let it get you down. Amid all the abuse you begin to gain confidence. They can't bluff you anymore. Maybe it's like it is with a writer. A writer writes for his readers, but works for his editor. A referee works for his boss and nobody else."

"The players may hate my guts," Hood states. "I don't know and I don't care. There's a few of them I don't like either. All I want from them is respect.

Ex-Ranger Curt Bennett pulls off a cross-check, a hook, a trip and interference in one motion. Of the four, interference is the most difficult to call since it happens on most plays in front of the net.

"There are all kinds of players," says Bill Chadwick, a member of the Hockey Hall of Fame and one of the best referees in the game's history. "There's class guys and cheap-shot artists, crybabies and whiners, grumblers and complainers. Somebody like Howe, he never said much at all. He didn't have to. He was a mean bastard, and that look of disgust he'd give you made you want to crawl into the ice.

"Rocket Richard was a fiery guy, a helluva competitor. He'd do anything to win, and browbeating a referee was hardly beneath him. Ted Lindsay was one of the cheap-shot artists. He liked to embarrass you, make you look bad. Like, on a whistle, shooting the puck down to the other end of the ice. Guys like Richard and Lindsay, I'd slap them with a misconduct the very first time I saw them every year, just to let them know I was around. All they had to do was blink and they were gone.

"Lou Fontinato, the defenseman for the Rangers and Montreal, pulled temper tantrums when he'd get a penalty—and he got a lot of 'em. Lou jumped up and down, a kid who couldn't have his way. He did it so much they called him 'Leapin' Louie.' Well Leapin' Louie only leaped once on me, because when he came down he had a misconduct."

Harris thinks a lot depends upon the mood the players are in. "It's just like a guy coming to the office hung over, or after having had a fight with his wife. Players are human beings. They have feelings. They aren't just objects, although it may look that way from the balcony or from the way they're with one team one day and then with another very shortly afterward.

"If players come to the rink in a bad mood, the least little thing can ignite them, set them off. Other nights you could hit them over the head with a stick and they wouldn't blink. Personally, I've found players particularly testy on Sunday nights, when they've been up traveling the night after a Saturday night game."

"The first five minutes of the game are the key," says Friday. "You look for that first good penalty and then, damn it, you call it. You can't let it go. If you do, then another good penalty comes along and maybe you let it go because you didn't call the first one. Then the players see what's going on. They go a little fur-

Above: Keith Magnuson rides around the corner with Henri Richard while veteran ref John Ashley watches carefully but impassively. *Opposite:* Friday dramatizes one of his calls for a less-than-entertained Dave Keon.

ther, a little further, and before you know it you've got real trouble on your hands. All because you didn't call that first good penalty."

Ashley agrees. "Trouble usually follows a pattern of events. First it's the body. Maybe they're hitting pretty good out there. Then they start yapping back and forth, and that's when they get that screwy look in their eyes. . . ."

Many fans must wonder how much profanity is used on the ice and whether it's permitted. "Sure there's cussing out there," Harris allows. "It's just like it is anywhere men get together. I call it dressing-room talk. I take it in stride. I mean, you hit a guy with a penalty and he's not going to say 'Thank you.'

"About the only time I'll give someone a misconduct is when he tries to make a fool out of me, tries to embarrass me in front of the other players and the crowd. If he's shouting so everyone can hear, waving his arms all over the place, I'll give him a misconduct . . . fast. And if I ask a guy what he said—and he's stupid enough to say it again—of course I'll give him ten minutes."

"If they jaw too much it's going to cost 'em dough," says Friday. "When you call a penalty, that's it. They can have their say, but enough's enough.

You're the guy who's in charge, you're the guy who knows the rules, and the sooner they realize it the better.

"That old pocketbook, it's a great equalizer. Look at Stan Mikita. I'd like to have a nickel for every dollar he was fined his first few years in the league. Stan just couldn't keep his mouth shut. He always had to have the last word, and it cost him a lotta dough. But Stan learned. He'll still have his say out there, but now he knows when to stop."

"You can't have rabbit ears out there," Hood concurs. "You can't go looking for trouble. A lot of it, you've just got to let it run off. There are times somebody can get you upset, but you can't take it personally. You've got to keep that straight face. You can't show anger, disgust or whatever. But if they keep it up, they go. After a while they learn how far you'll let them push you.

"I try not to say much at all out there. It's not good policy. You say something to them and they're liable to come right back at you. It's like Scotty tells us. Set your standards and stick to them. If the language is strong right after a call is made, of course the player has to go. But if a cuss word creeps in when a question is being asked in a generally busi-

nesslike manner, you've got to use your discretion."

"You can't penalize a guy for using his normal language," says Chadwick. "With me I really didn't care what he said to me, just so he didn't say it with somebody else within earshot.

"I remember one time I really got in a good lick, though. It was during a game in Chicago, back when the fans used to play cards in the balcony between periods or during stoppages in play. They'd bring decks of cards held together with rubber bands.

"I called a penalty on John Mariucci [now assistant general manager of the Minnesota North Stars] and John came right back at me. I gave him a misconduct. That really made him hot. He was fuming as he skated to the box, and as he went in he slammed the door behind him.

"Just about then a deck of cards came sailing down from the balcony and splattered all over the ice. After picking up a handful, I was skating over to the scorer's bench, and I looked at John, in the box, still fuming. So as I skated past I tossed the cards in his lap and said, 'Here John. You might as well start a game of solitaire. You'll be in there long enough.' "

This is typical of the dry humor that often occurs during the course of a game. But because of their "official" nature referees usually receive more than they give.

"Howe was a great needler," remembers Frank Udvari, one of the NHL's best referees until an eye injury suffered in a 1968 automobile accident ended his career. "One time he just skated up and said, 'Frank, you're the second best referee in the league.' Then, before I could say anything, he comes back with, 'Everybody else is tied for first.' "

"I'll never forget the game when Gary Bergman of the Red Wings took a slap shot in the forehead," says Harris. "It was between Toronto and Detroit in Detroit on New Year's night. Somebody wound up and fired from the point and Bergman goes down like he's pole-axed. He's knocked cold, stretched out on the ice. We were all pretty concerned, 'cause he wasn't moving or anything, and trainers are working over him, towels are full of blood. My linesmen and I are standing there when Howe skates by. 'A beer says it's less than fifteen,' he says.

" 'Whaaaat . . . ?' I said.

" 'Stitches,' he says. 'A beer says it doesn't take fifteen stitches to close the cut.'

"Well here's Bergman laid out, blood pouring from his head. Some of us are almost wondering if

A scramble in front of California's goal cannot produce a goal while Detroit's Delvecchio is in the crease. Referees dread this kind of situation.

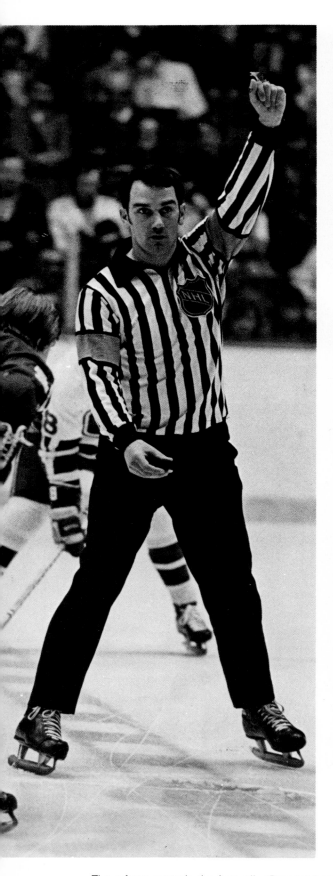

The referee controls the face-off. "Respect from players takes time,"
says Wally Harris. "You have to earn their respect." *Opposite:*
Matt Pavelich and Bill Friday attempt to earn the respect of Rod Gilbert.

he's going to live . . . and a minute later Howe, Neil Armstrong and I are betting beers on how many stitches he'll get. I remember Howe took fifteen or less, Neil had seventeen and I took sixteen 'cause it was in the middle.

"They carry Bergman off and he doesn't come back for the rest of the period. Second period, no Bergman. We were starting to wonder when, about halfway through the third period, Bergman comes out and sits down at the end of the Red Wing bench. He's groggy as hell, got a towel wrapped around his neck, and there are stitches running across his forehead.

"Within five minutes all three of us have skated by the end of the bench. 'Gosh Bergy, that's a pretty bad cut. How many stitches, huh . . . ?'

"I'm sure Bergman never dreamed so many people cared. As far as I know he never found out why we were so interested. By the way, Armstrong won with seventeen."

"One time," says Frank Udvari, "the Black Hawks were playing the Leafs in Toronto. It was a Saturday night and the game was telecast on 'Hockey Night in Canada.' Who gets into a fight but Phil Esposito, then with Chicago, and Carl Brewer of the Leafs. Neither one has a reputation for liking to fight, and as they're

flailing away they're almost looking over their shoulders for somebody to break them up. But I always felt that if two evenly matched guys wanted to fight, let 'em fight. And these guys sure weren't going to hurt each other.

"After a while, the linesmen piled in and got them separated. But then Esposito sees that Brewer is bleeding from above an eye. Suddenly Phil's a mad dog! I don't know why; maybe the fact that the game was on national television had something to do with it. Anyway he proceeds to give Brewer a pretty good licking. When they're finally broken up and heading for the penalty box, Brewer skates past me, blood streaming down his face, and says, 'Hell, Frank. Why do you always have to experiment on me?' "

Veteran Bruce Hood raised his left hand. "See that?" he said, pointing to the scar which extended from the top of the hand, around the base of the thumb and all the way to the wrist at the bottom of the hand. "If a plastic surgeon hadn't been sitting with the Bruins' trainer one night, I'd have lost my thumb."

The Oakland Seals were playing in Boston when Carol Vadnais, then with Oakland, locked skates with a Bruin in front of the net. Both men tumbled to the ice, and when the action swept into the other end, Hood skated over to help them out.

"I could see that all I had to do was lift Vadnais's skate up and out," Hood said, "and I was just reaching to do it when he suddenly jerked his foot. The skate came free, and the blade sliced between my thumb and forefinger, almost to the wrist. The thumb was just dangling there. It looked like it would fall off. But when we got to the dressing room, the surgeon was there, and, as you can see, he did a pretty good job on it."

With little protective equipment and the necessity for intense concentration on the game itself, officials are even more susceptible to injury than the players. True, players don't run at or start fights with officials, but pucks whizzing at 100 miles per hour and high-sticking combatants jamming them into the boards are certain to extract a toll.

Scheduling is so tight, however, that on a given night all three officials may be skating hurt. Pulled muscles, dislocated shoulders and cracked ribs are common ("Have you ever tried to blow a whistle with cracked ribs?" asks Hood). Rare is the night in which any official is 100 percent healthy.

"I remember Eddie Powers," says Neil Armstrong. "He had this bad back for years. It had to have constant support, so he had it taped for games and slept on a hard bed. But on trips he used two boards fastened together, one to support his back, the other to give him something hard to sit on. He refereed with that bad back right up until he quit.

"One thing that amazes me," Armstrong continues, "is why more linesmen aren't hurt on slap shots from just inside the blue line. You've got to sit there, with your nose on that line, to make sure the puck doesn't leave the zone. But at the same time, these point men are winding up and blasting away. I don't know why the linesman isn't smacked in the face with the backswing. I'm sure it will happen one of these days. It's like looking down the barrel of a gun."

While most NHL officials who are injured have nothing more than their private pain to show for it, Armstrong became known to fans around the league as "that tall guy with the cast on his arm" during the latter half of the 1971–72 season. His injury, which resulted in a cast from the hand to the elbow of his right arm, occurred during a game in February between the Philadelphia Flyers and the Vancouver Canucks. As Vancouver's Pat Quinn carried the Flyers'

Opposite: New York's Billy Fairbairn incurs a boarding penalty. *Above:* Whitey Stapleton argues over a penalty with Bill Friday. *Left:* Bill Friday halts play.

Gary Dornhoeffer into the boards, the heel of Dornhoeffer's stick came thudding down upon the hand of Armstrong, who, with both hands planted on the dasher, was leaping to avoid the colliding players. "It cracked one of the bones in the hand, between the thumb and the forefinger," Armstrong said. "It's a little bone, really, but it happens to be the only one in the body that doesn't receive much blood. As a result, the healing process is very slow.

"It didn't bother me, except when I lifted a cup of coffee or opened a door. Then the pain was unbearable. The cure? A cast for four to six months. All for a little bone like that."

"The thing is, you're so involved in the game you often don't see trouble coming," says Hood. "Like when I got my nose broken in the old Madison Square Garden. I thought I'd been hit by something thrown from the crowd. I was off to the side of the Rangers' net when Dale Rolfe, then with Los Angeles, fired from the point. Then the lights went out. The next thing I knew I was laying on my back and blood was pouring from somewhere on my face. What had happened was the puck had deflected off Vic Hadfield's skate, right between my eyes. I never saw it."

It was seven o'clock now, and the cocktail lounge of the Statler Hilton was filled with the loud talk and laughter of people toasting the arrival of the weekend: in an hour, dinner with the wife at the Italian place . . . tomorrow, a day with the kids and a night at the club . . . and Sunday, who knows . . .

But Bruce Hood was in no mood to celebrate anything. In an hour he would go for a brief skate with Armstrong and Pavelich to loosen up and then have a steak somewhere. After that he would try to get some sleep. On Saturday the waiting would get worse, so he would try to think of other things. The game of squash with Frank Udvari at noon would help. But Saturday was going to be a long day, that was for sure; the butterflies in Bruce Hood's stomach wouldn't turn into bats overnight.

Early Sunday afternoon, the sun was shining brightly, and the temperature had reached the low eighties in New York. But it was quite cool in Madison Square Garden, and the usual sellout crowd of stockbrokers, ad men, models and executive secretaries, sensing the importance of the contest, was quick to fill the seats. As game time approached and the CBS-TV announcers high above the ice smoothed stray hairs into place, the atmosphere inside the huge arena had become an expectant mixture of crowd noise, organ music and scattered blasts on air horns.

At 2:01 P.M., the small door at the northwest end of the playing surface swung open and Hood, Armstrong and Pavelich skated onto the ice, sleek and trim in their tailored black-and-white uniforms. Hood, square-shouldered, face expressionless, was greeted with boos. But as quickly as his presence was noted it was forgotten in the thunderous wave of cheers and applause that engulfed the Rangers as, wearing their basic white with red and blue trim, they appeared from beneath the stands at center ice. Boos once again filled the building as the Bruins, ominous in their yellow-on-black, followed the New York club onto the ice.

Hood blew his whistle, signaling that the ice be cleared. It was obvious already how desperately each team wanted the game. ("You could see it in their faces," the referee would say later. "Each man had that cold, hard look in his face. The only time you see that look is when something big is at stake.") The Rangers, 5–2 victors on Thursday night, needed a win to send the series back to Boston all tied at two games apiece. The Bruins, on the other hand, had played well all season in Madison Square Garden and were fully aware that one more victory in New York would enable them to wrap up the Stanley Cup in the Boston Garden Tuesday night. (As Boston's Derek Sanderson had been quoted in the papers, "Why should we bother coming back down here again? It's nothing but a zoo anyway.")

Then the game was on—and Bruce Hood lost no time establishing himself. With barely a minute gone, Boston's Phil Esposito sent his stick and elbows high in the air trying to shed the shadow of New York's Walt Tkaczuk. Hood, his right arm stabbing the air, sent the big Bruin center off at 1:24 for high-sticking.

On the ensuing face-off at center ice, Sanderson, out to kill the penalty, won the draw and fired the puck into the corner to the left of Ranger goalie Ed Giacomin. No sooner did Bobby Rousseau retrieve it than Sanderson was on top of him, first shoving his smaller opponent with both forearms—then, gloves gone, pummeling him about the white helmet. Rousseau had no choice but to retaliate, and at 1:39 Hood gave both players five-minute major penalties for fighting. In the supercharged atmosphere, Hood already faced an uphill battle in maintaining control of the game.

Less than two minutes later, he had his hands full again. New York's Gary Doak, watching Don Marcotte

Vic Hadfield accidentally connects with the wrong man *(opposite left)*, Alex Delvecchio argues with Wally Harris *(opposite top)* and Matt Pavelich *(opposite bottom)*. Hadfield was fined heavily for his actions.

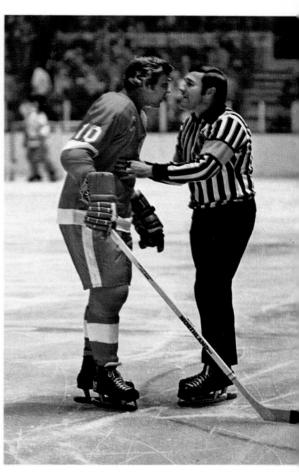

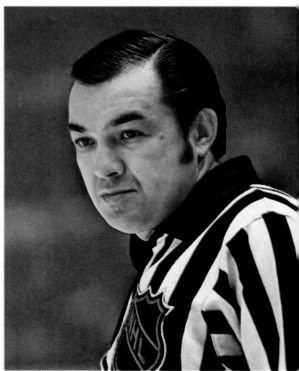

49

building up a head of steam on a rush into the Rangers' zone, countered with a move that fit somewhere into the broad category labeled "interference". Frustrated, Marcotte replied with a high stick. Both dropped their gloves and sticks and assumed boxing stances, but Armstrong and Pavelich separated them before a blow was landed. Doak and Marcotte both received two-minute minor penalties as expected, but then, mysteriously, Ed Westfall of the Bruins was sent off too.

"So much of it is just psychological warfare," Hood said later. "Westfall rarely argues on the current penalty. He's always looking to the next one. When I sent Esposito off, Westfall was right at my elbow. I told him to get lost, that there was to be no talking to the officials during the play-offs and he knew it. But as soon as I sent Marcotte off with Doak, he was right there at my elbow again. I had no choice but to chase him."

With the game only 3:20 old, the penalty box was occupied by four black shirts and two white. "It was a game in which you had no choice but to take charge early or forget it," Hood said later.

The next few minutes were relatively tranquil, and shortly after the teams had returned to full strength, Bobby Orr was knifing between two Ranger defenders with the puck on his stick, courtesy of a neat pass from Mike Walton at the New York blue line. Orr took his time and fired the puck high into the corner over the left shoulder of Giacomin and the Bruins led, 1–0.

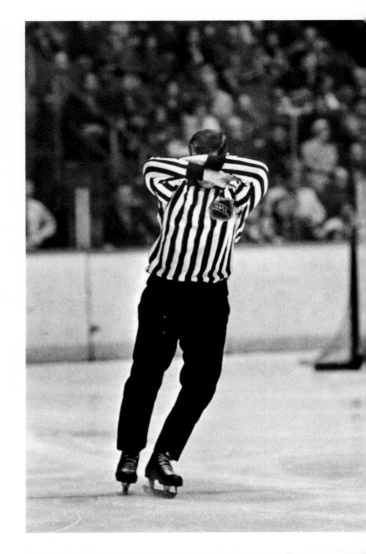

But the Rangers fought back and two minutes later rookie Gene Carr was charging behind the Boston net in pursuit of Don Awrey. Both men clanged against the glass in a tangle of sticks and elbows, and Hood's arm shot into the air again. When Carr discovered that he was the only one getting a penalty, he promptly dispatched his gloves and started a fight with Awrey. Hood sent both off at 7:21 for fighting, not forgetting to give Carr an extra two minutes for high-sticking.

As it turned out, those two minutes were the difference in the game. Pouring on the pressure right from the face-off, Boston controlled the puck in the New York zone—and 56 seconds later Orr drilled a low shot under Giacomin's pad from 35 feet away. With the Rangers down 2–0, the huge crowd fell silent.

The Rangers, however, were aroused. Battling back like a fighter all at once smeared with his own blood, even smaller New Yorkers like Rousseau and Bruce MacGregor took runs at the bigger Bruins. The

Icing *(opposite top)* is an easy call for which no penalty is given, but more difficult are the calls that could result from Dale Rolfe's confrontation with Wayne Cashman, 12 *(above),* or the check *(left)* that stifles an attack coming at full speed.

tempo of the game increased and as the action moved from one end of the ice to the other—the throng cheering, moaning, then cheering again—the contest seemed to be building toward an early climax. The Rangers were pressing, but another goal for the Bruins would mean an almost insurmountable 3–0 lead. Then again, a New York score would put the Rangers right back into the game. The roaring crowd seemed torn between two choices: slowing things down and waiting for a break or going all-out for the next goal.

In the midst of it, Hood, his mouth in the usual tight, thin line, was keeping the game solidly in hand. It had not gotten away from him early, and it wasn't going to escape him now. And if he could maintain order now, the chances were that the second and third periods would be easier. At 9:45 Hood caught Esposito holding and Ted Irvine charging, and at 11:44 he sent Walton off for slashing. The score was still 2–0, Boston.

"The period was really quite basic from an officiating standpoint," Hood would say later. "The penal-

ties were obvious, flagrant. All I had to do was raise my arm. It wasn't like the close hook or close interference at center ice. . . ."

With four minutes remaining in the period, New York coach Emile Francis sent scrappy Glen Sather, an ex-Bruin, over the boards for the first time. Fifteen seconds later Brad Park cruised up to Orr at the New York blue line and delivered a resounding *thwack* to the Boston star's stick. The message was obvious— but Orr caught Park by surprise when he ducked under Park's fists and sent him onto the ice with a driving tackle. Then Sather and John McKenzie were tumbling to the ice, gloves and fists flying. When everyone was finally sorted out, Hood awarded each a five-minute major for fighting and tagged McKenzie with a ten-minute misconduct—not for saying too much, but for what he had said. After Dallas Smith received a hooking penalty at 18:28, the period ended with three Bruins and two Rangers in the penalty box. In the first 20 minutes of the game, Hood had given out 76 minutes in penalties.

"As we went back to the dressing room, Matt

Opposite: Cashman attacks Tkaczuk, impeded only by strong-willed Neil Armstrong. Occasionally, a referee will allow two combatants to fight it out alone. *Above:* Joe Watson, 14, hooks Bobby Rousseau, 22.

and Neil and I were saying, hell, there was no way the teams could keep up that pace," Hood recalled. "Oh, they could keep it up all right, but they'd drop dead. We talked over the first period and felt we'd done a pretty good job. We had hopes things might be a little easier because of it."

As it turned out, the officials were indeed rewarded. At 0:22 of the second period Hood dispatched Ken Hodge of Boston for hooking, and five minutes later Carol Vadnais of Boston and Vic Hadfield went off for fighting and the Bruins' Ace Bailey for elbowing. Play leveled out after that, but at 15:33 Hood whistled Walton off for high-sticking.

Exactly one minute later, the puck was billowing the net behind Giacomin after Orr, out to kill the penalty, sent Marcotte in on a strong rush from the left side. The score seemed to doom the Rangers, who appeared content simply to go through the motions the rest of the period. But the Bruins got sloppy in their own end, and when Irvine whipped the puck past Ed Johnston at 18:38 the Rangers went off with new life, trailing only 3–1.

Compared to the first two periods, the third was like a stroll in the park for Hood. Boston, brought out of the clouds by Irvine's goal, was determined to protect its lead—and that meant *no penalties*. The Rangers, just as determined at least to tie the game and send it into overtime, knew that the best way to approach the task was at full strength. At 9:01 Hood sent Stemkowski of New York off for an obvious tripping violation, but the Rangers fought off the Bruin power play with little difficulty. Boston, it was clear, did not feel any more goals were necessary. At 15:02 Hood caught Awrey hooking in front of the Boston net; but the Rangers, tense now, never could get their power plays moving. When Hodge took a bad penalty (tripping) at 17:18, New York's Seiling laced a low shot under Johnston's leg from 30 feet out. The

Above: Ranger Bruce MacGregor, in crease, scores against Boston on a deflection as referee Hood signals that MacGregor was indeed the man who scored. *Opposite:* Phil Roberto versus Bill Friday.

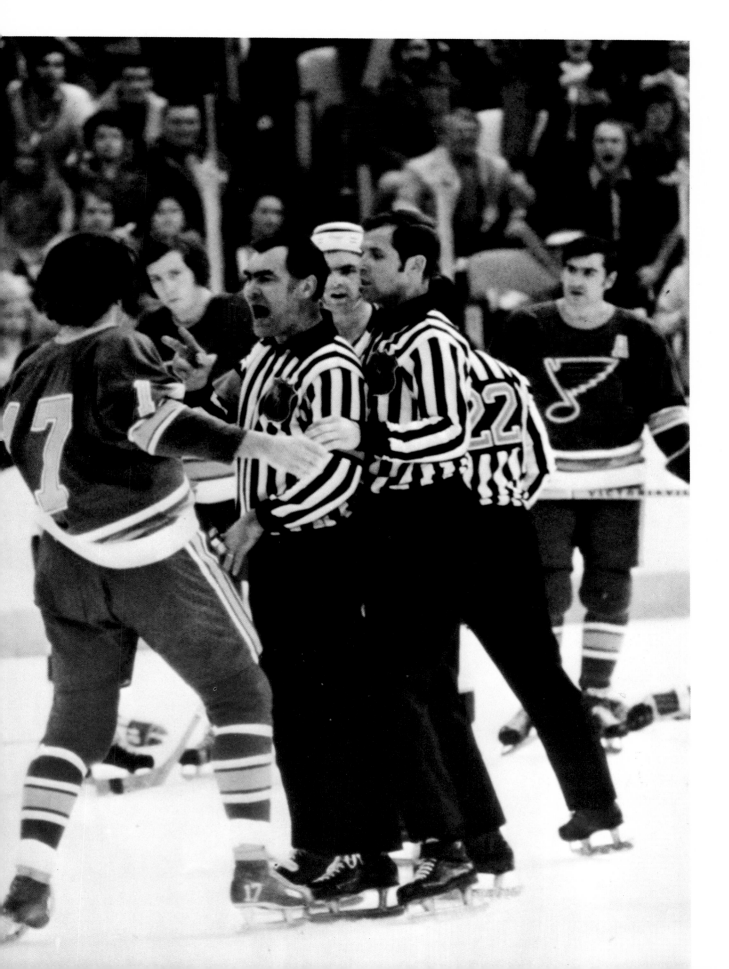

score was now 3–2, Boston, with 1:25 to go.

With the crowd suddenly back to life, Hood watched the Rangers jockey for an opportunity to pull Giacomin. Boston, breaking up the new Rangers' passing combinations at center ice, proceeded to dump the puck back into the New York zone. A minute and 10 seconds were left . . . a minute 5 . . . "One minute remaining in the game!" a voice boomed over the public address system.

Fifty-five seconds . . . high above the balcony at each end of the building, red neon numerals flashed the contest closer to its conclusion. Fifty seconds. . . .

With 47 seconds to go, the Rangers finally managed to fire the puck into the Boston zone. As Jean Ratelle, Hadfield and Rod Gilbert charged after it, Giacomin raced to the Rangers' bench and Francis sent a sixth attacker over the boards. Thirty-eight seconds . . .

With a half-minute left in the game Hadfield found

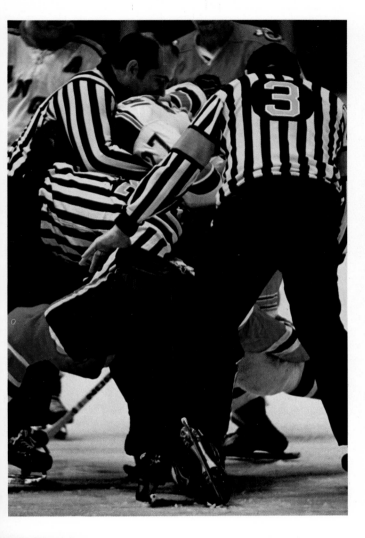

Clockwise from above: Keith Magnuson trips Rousseau; Bill Friday, 3, stays on top of things; Art Skov listens patiently; linesman Willard Norris scales plexiglass, out of harm's way.

the puck on his stick about 15 feet out and to the left of the Boston goal. Johnston, caught by surprise, could not cover the half of the net nearest Hadfield— but the big Ranger forward shot wide. The puck rebounded off the boards behind the goal, and as Hood moved nimbly out of the way, Orr rushed back to regain possession for Boston. Twenty-five seconds later, the game was over.

The door to the officials' dressing room was closed when Bill Friday, who would referee Tuesday night's game in Boston, arrived in a maroon-and-white checked sport jacket, maroon slacks, maroon-and-white print shirt, paisley tie and white shoes. As he rapped his knuckles on the steel door, Friday was asked what it was like to observe a game such as the one he had just seen.

"It's murder," he said. "In your own mind you're working it right along with the guy on the ice. You feel the pressure as much as he does, because we're all in this together and you want to see him do well.

"Down there, on the ice, most of your moves and decisions are instinctive. You make them almost without thinking. But when you're watching the other guy do it, all you can really do is think and worry. And the tension is worse, because you're not skating any of it off. All you can do is pace up and down somewhere. You sure as hell can't just sit there."

The door opened, and Friday walked in to offer a hand to Hood, who was sipping soda from a paper cup. Scotty Morrison and Frank Udvari were already in the room, obviously pleased at the way the game had been handled.

"A helluva game," Friday said, offering his congratulations. "Just a helluva game."

"They really went at it that first period, didn't they?" Hood said.

"A ball-buster, that's what it was," said Friday, shaking his head. "A real ball-buster."

As a closer discussion of the game went on around him, Hood put the paper cup on a bench and slipped into a light-brown sport jacket. From across the room, Frank Udvari winked as if to say, "Well done."

Bruce Hood smiled broadly. His ordeal was over until a new season began. It was moments such as these, satisfying moments when one was accepting congratulations from peers and superiors alike, that made all the abuse worthwhile.

During moments like these, a referee in the National Hockey League isn't a different breed of cat at all.

Above: Bruce Hood leans over the glass to explain the penalty. He says, "For me, the loneliness and the waiting are the toughest things about being a referee in the National Hockey League."
Left: Bill Friday fights loneliness his way.

Expansion hasn't changed just the geography of the National Hockey League—it has altered the game's basic strategy too. Before expansion, when each team played each of the other five 14 times during the season, players got to know their opponents from A to Z. Today, with 16 teams in the league already and further expansion anticipated, players scarcely remember names, let alone individual talents.

For instance, in 1972, a new club, Atlanta, is at Buffalo on opening night. It's certain that the next time the two teams play, Atlanta will be a different hockey club. They'll have made some deals, brought players up, sent others down. As a result, almost anything Buffalo might do to gear for Atlanta opening night is a waste of time.

You used to be able to compile a pretty good book on a club. You knew their style, whether they liked to carry the puck in or shoot it in, what guys you had to take out of a play. I'd put a checking line against Gordie Howe's line when we were playing Detroit, or Jean Beliveau's line against Montreal, and that was the extent of our game plan. Of course, on some nights Howe simply controlled a game, so that it didn't matter who you had out there. Before I joined the Toronto Maple Leafs, they always put a fellow named Bob Davidson out there to check Rocket Richard of the Canadiens. Davidson was a big, strong guy, a good checker they felt could do the job on the Rocket. Well, one night in the play-offs, Rocket scored five goals with Davidson on him and Montreal won, 5–1. Bob has never lived it down.

Nevertheless, you knew your opponents well enough to match lines with them. As in football, you watched films of your next opponent and sort of laid out a game plan for that particular club. In Toronto we used films to a greater extent than did any other club. Then we went from films to video tape. Toward the end of my tenure with the Leafs, I had a video machine in a room near the bench. Following a controversial play, I'd duck into that room, throw the replay on the machine and know exactly what had happened. Then I could come out and raise all sorts of hell with the referee. It was an unfair advantage, of course, but if the referee looked over and noticed I wasn't saying anything, he knew he was doing all right. But if he was unsure about a play and looked over to see that I wasn't behind the bench, he knew I

Preceding pages and above: Action in front of the net in the area known as the "slot." From here a team often scores, and hitting is essential.

was going to be down his back in a few seconds. I had a lot of fun with that.

With expansion you don't have the time to lay out a complete game plan. If we're playing Saturday night in St. Louis and at home Sunday night, we're on a plane right after the St. Louis game and don't get to Buffalo until two o'clock in the morning. There's no time to have a meeting. With a game at seven o'clock that night, I'll tell the team to report at five-thirty. What chance do I have to introduce a game plan? I don't even have time to show films or the video tape of the game in St. Louis. All I can do is try to get my club mentally ready to play another hockey game. You have to be more general in your approach. If we're playing Boston, we know we're going to have to play a fine game, but the only specific thing we'll do is pray that Bobby Orr misses the plane.

The time you can approach things right is when you have three days off—say a Sunday night game followed by a Thursday night game—which is rare. My players are coming in on Monday anyway, so if

they happened to play badly the night before, I might say, "All right, you're going to watch that game from beginning to end, it was so bad. And furthermore, you're going to pay to see it. The fans paid to see it, so I'm going to charge you twenty-five dollars apiece to see it, and you had better be here."

Of course, you never charge them. It's just a gimmick to show how upset you are, and you might tell the newspapers about it. But they do watch the whole game. You can stop the tape and go back over the things they did right or wrong. Then you can take them onto the ice and illustrate firsthand what they have just watched. Follow that with some solid work-outs Tuesday and Wednesday, and by Thursday night they're not only rested but also ready, both physically and mentally, to play hockey.

Before expansion, the NHL usually played Satur-day and Sunday nights and Wednesday and Thursday nights. That left you with some pretty good days for practice. And because you had probably played your next opponent only a week or 10 days ago, you could

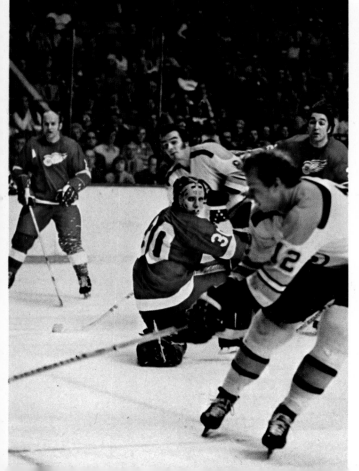

Clockwise from opposite: Buffalo's Lorentz, 8, and
Meehan get position on Philadelphia; Toronto's
Ellis is taken from play; Blues' Dupont, 3, picks up
a rebound and starts up ice; Boston takes advantage
of its muscle—Hodge shoots and Cashman rebounds.

refer back to that game and point out how you did this against them or how they did that against you. But today, playing 78 games and traveling from coast to coast like a vagabond, you just can't worry about how your next opponent's been going. You've got to worry about yourself.

Now in the play-offs you know you're going to be meeting a particular club at least four times in succession, so you have a better opportunity to prepare for them. But even then, the league has you playing back-to-back games the first week—say, Wednesday-Thursday and Saturday-Sunday with Friday off for travel—so you're almost in the same straits as in the regular season. If your guys play badly on Wednesday night, you haven't got a chance to straighten them out for Thursday. I argue this up and down, but nobody will ever listen to me. They say we've got to get the first week over with. I say if it's worth playing, it's worth playing right. And that means having at least a day between games so that you can get some coaching done.

For instance, that game Toronto played in Boston in the 1969 play-offs, when we were trounced 11–0, was on a Wednesday night. Pat Quinn of the Leafs creamed Bobby Orr coming out of the Boston end. A big fight developed, and a fan grabbed Forbes Kennedy over the glass, and there was almost a riot. Kennedy was ultimately suspended. The papers described what an ugly scene it had been and how much worse it could have been. There was no telling what might happen on Thursday night, they said. My guys read the papers the next day and went into the game that night apprehensive. We lost, 7–0. If I'd had a day in between, they could have read the papers, but then we would have gone to practice. Calmly, quietly, we would have talked about what had happened, and they could have skated out their anxiety.

The important thing today is that you yourself are ready to play. You must emphasize your own system and not worry about that of your opponent. Besides, hockey is such a fast game that there aren't as many set plays as in football or basketball. Hockey is, for the most part, spontaneous action—and although that's what can tear a coach's heart out at times, it's also what makes the game so exciting to watch. Each club has a general system, and the one I've always used is very basic, very simple. There's an old adage in hockey that if you take care of your own end of the rink, the other end will take care of itself. So what you work on more than anything else is

Though working the puck in close is the best way to produce a goal, the slap shot is a dangerous weapon. At 120 mph, the puck is often just a blur.

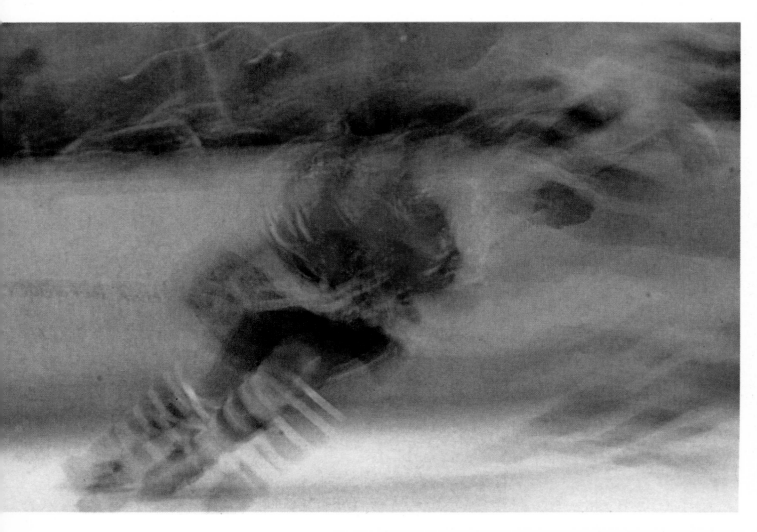

Constant movement and aggressiveness are the keys to a successful club. *Above:* A Chicago wing whirls to backcheck. Gil Perreault *(right)* wings across the ice to dog a loose puck. *Opposite:* Dennis Hull plants himself near Villemure.

eliminating those costly mistakes in your own end.

Where most clubs get in trouble is in bringing the puck out of their own end. In the years we were winning the Stanley Cups, Toronto basically had the defenseman behind the net with the puck, and he would attempt to get it to the other defenseman in the corner, who would then move it up through the middle to our centerman circling. The last year we won the Cup, 1967, we were sending the center behind the net to either pick up the puck or leave it for the defenseman. Whether to pick it up or leave it was strictly up to the centerman; he was looking at the play in front of the net, and when he thought the forechecker would try to take him (the center) out of the play, which is what the forechecker should do, he left the puck for the defenseman and kept moving toward the boards. Then, when the defenseman came out with the puck, the forechecker had to make a decision: either stay with the centerman or stop and take the defenseman with the puck. If the forechecker stayed with the centerman, the defenseman carried the puck right up through the middle. If the forechecker took the defenseman, he passed off to the centerman along the boards, and away they went.

Basically, however, my strategy is to keep moving. In other words, as soon as you get the puck, turn on the offense. As soon as your opponent gets it, switch immediately to defense. Being the stickler for defense that I am, my players have very definite things they are supposed to do when the other team has the puck. Mostly, they have to pick up certain men. But when we get the puck, I want them to exploit as quickly as possible the relative positions on the ice, the weaknesses and personnel of the opposition. They aren't to stop and set anything up. They *move*. If the other club is caught with three men in our zone, we get the hell out of there fast and try to develop a three-on-two break. If they're overcommitted to the left side of the rink, we try to get the puck to one of our guys on the right side.

Obviously, there can be no set pattern to this offense. Everything depends upon the individual skills and personalities of my players. I don't insist that they stay on their wings on offense, but if they do, so much the better, because then everybody has an idea of where everybody else is. As long as they don't get into trouble defensively, my players are free to exploit —within reason—the other club. Gordie Howe was notorious for roaming all over the ice when he played in Detroit, but at the same time the team covered for

Left: Vancouver's Gerry O'Flaherty challenges Rod Gilbert at the blue line. *Above:* Buffalo practices a clearing play. Center comes behind the net, but defenseman holds the puck. When center is in position, defenseman starts up ice with options.

him so well that it didn't matter where he was on the exchange of the puck.

The reason I emphasize constant movement for my players is that when they stop, the game becomes one of checkers. The other club has a chance to form up against us. We're starting from scratch, and so are they. Everything's equal, except that we have the puck. If we set up with our left defenseman behind the net and our right defenseman in the right corner, they will send their left wing in to take our right defenseman. Their center, or forechecker, takes our defenseman behind the net, their right winger takes our centerman circling in the slot and their right defenseman takes our left wing. When you stop, there just isn't that much you can do that's different from what anyone else does.

The New York Rangers, for example, don't ordinarily send their centerman behind the net; he usually circles at the side and comes out from the corner. I don't know why they do it that way. Maybe Emile Francis just feels that his players won't get clawed up behind the net and that he's eliminating the pos-

sibility of confusion over who's going to come out with the puck. But it's still not that different from the way anyone else does it.

Sometimes you alter your routine. In 1967, we could put the defenseman in the corner or out in front of the net, where he was supposed to interfere with the forechecker, and give the guy behind the net a chance to get going. Our personnel was such then that we could do it either way. But about a month before the play-offs, we changed from going to the defenseman in the corner to having the center come

Opposite: Minnesota and its fans exult as a deflection goes in against St. Louis in Cup game. *Below:* St. Louis Blue Garry Unger flips puck past Minnesotan Danny Grant. *Bottom:* Wayne Cashman tries to beat Gary Bergman to puck as Phil Esposito waits in the slot.

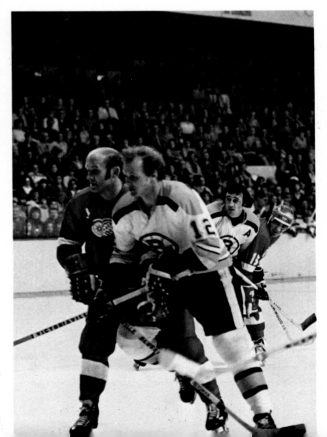

behind the net and pick up the puck. It just seemed to fit the players we had, particularly free-wheeling centers like Red Kelly, Dave Keon and Pete Stemkowski. These men were expert stickhandlers and could skate well. We won the Cup that year.

On defense, everybody has a specific job to do. Depending on the opponent, you can send in one or two men to forecheck the other team in its own zone. I'll never send two men in all helter-skelter. Two men will go in, but the man closer to the puck plays it. If the puck comes loose, the second man has a decision to make: If he feels he has a 50–50 chance or better of getting the puck, he goes for it. If it's 60–40 or worse against him, he's to forget the puck and come back with their wingman. Both forecheckers' assignments are interchangeable. If the center goes in to play the puck, the wing picks up the center's man and vice versa. But when two men get caught, and sometimes that happens, the third forward, the one who's backchecking, never takes the puck carrier. The puck carrier will ultimately be taken by a defenseman. If a backchecker takes the puck carrier, you're going to have two men on one, leaving somebody open.

Sometimes you have players that don't fit the pattern of sending two men with interchangeable responsibilities. Then I might tell one guy to do the backchecking all the time. He'll cruise into the slot in front of their net, but he'll always be ready to come back. That gives us two forwards and two defensemen on their three-man rush. My method of sending two men in, but with only the nearer man playing the puck and the other playing the percentages if it comes free, is a fairly disciplined way of forechecking. Here, I think, we differ from every other club in the league.

When you're on offense, you can either carry the puck into the other team's zone or shoot it in. Everything depends upon your personnel. Most clubs today, especially Detroit, like to shoot the puck into the corner and chase it. One wingman takes the defenseman out of the play, and the centerman comes in and takes the puck. The third man moves into the slot. In theory, the man who shoots the puck in is supposed to be stopped at the blue line; the defenseman who kept him from carrying the puck in is supposed to take him out of the play.

If you are fortunate enough to have a player like our Gil Perreault, who is capable of carrying the puck into the other team's zone by himself, you're that much better off. You aren't risking giving the puck

Top left: Falling Butch Goring throws the puck in, a popular tactic among today's teams. *Top right:* Bobby Schmautz fires from the blue line, but the shot is blocked immediately. *Right:* Jean Ratelle tries to split backcheckers Stan Mikita and Dennis Hull.

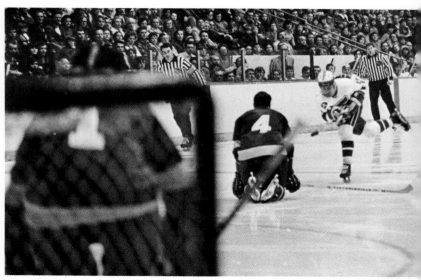

Left: Bobby Clarke, in perfect position, pounces on a rebound. *Top:* Ross Lonsberry, 18, is dumped by Larry Hillman. *Above:* Vic Hadfield breaks up ice.

away by shooting it. The Canadiens had such a player in Beliveau, the Red Wings in Howe. Boston has two today in Phil Esposito and Bobby Orr. When someone like that carries the puck in, he can draw the defense to him, set up a teammate and do almost a million other things, depending on how the play unfolds. It's a great advantage.

The idea of the game is five men up, five men back. The three forwards and two defensemen move as a unit; they don't let half the ice get between them. That's why the defensemen have to move up to the blue line both on offense and defense. They've got to help the forwards, and the forwards have got to come back and help them. When the forwards aren't coming back, the defensemen have to keep backing up, backing up, giving up ground in an attempt to cut down the angles. But the more they back up, the more room they're giving the other club.

I tell my defensemen, "*Use* that blue line; it's there to help you. Don't give it away." It's the same with the boards. "The boards can be your best friend out there," I tell them. "*Use* them. You give the puck to the boards, the boards give it back."

If the other club is coming at you with a three-man rush, they still can't cross that blue line until the puck does. So when that guy with the puck gets near the blue line, you try to check him or delay him. He's got to do something and do it fast. If he lets you tie him up, everybody else is going to be off-side. If he shoots it in, you've now got a chance to go back and get it or force a face-off. That's using the blue line to your advantage. Nobody did it better than the defensemen we had in Toronto when we won those three consecutive Stanley Cups—Tim Horton, Allan Stanley, Carl Brewer and Bobby Baun. They were probably the best defensive foursome any club has ever had.

Obviously, it doesn't make much difference who the coach is if a team has great hockey players. Great players will usually carry a team to the top regardless of what a coach does. The coach can only establish discipline and a system and adapt that system to his personnel. But if you're a coach, you're always trying to improve what you do. It was the same thing with those Green Bay football teams under Vince Lombardi. Everybody knew what they were going to do— they were going to run over you. There was no secret about it. But they did it so well, they couldn't be stopped. And they were always improving it. As far as I'm concerned, the same thing applies to hockey.

Another method of clearing the defensive zone is demonstrated by Buffalo as center takes puck from defenseman and initiates clearing play himself.

Since you know what you want to do, you set out to do it exceptionally well. From day one of training camp, you say to your players, "Here is the system. These are your responsibilities." Then you keep practicing the system over and over again until it becomes second nature. Your players will make mistakes. Hockey is a game of mistakes. But as with every other sport, the club that makes the fewest mistakes will come out on top.

I believe in being aggressive. When you're aggressive, at least you know what you're doing. In other words, if I'm coming out to hit you, I know exactly what I'm going to do. I'm not waiting for you to make a move so I can counter. I'd rather hit you first and worry about the consequences later. In the long run, the aggressor is going to have the edge. Toronto was an aggressive hockey club. They hit more than anyone else. We kept track of who did the hitting in every game. All successful clubs are aggressive.

For example, when the puck goes out to the point, my guy doesn't just skate out there and make a circle. He tries to knock the point man down. He flattens him for a couple of reasons. One, he's taken him out of the play. Suppose he gives up the puck and it goes to one of my players. Now my player comes out and, with this guy flat on his back, we've got a chance at a two-on-one break. Two, if we religiously take that man out every time, he's not going to be so anxious to make a play. He's not going to take that extra look, that extra second to set things up a little better. Instead, knowing that we're going to bang into him, he's going to get rid of the puck a little faster, increasing the chances he won't make a good pass or shot.

In Buffalo, we want our players to be aggressive. And we keep track of our "hits" here, just as I did in Toronto. Sure, we're an expansion club and it's an uphill fight, but if you stand around and wait for a club like Boston, they'll murder you.

If you're a coach, you're always looking for good, tough, aggressive hockey players, guys who don't lose their individual fights. Tim Horton is going to be very valuable to us this year, because after Horton goes into the corner with somebody, that guy doesn't come out. The puck may come out, but that guy doesn't. Then Horton comes out to help somebody who's having trouble. The puck won't go into the net by itself, and if you've got enough guys like Horton, there aren't going to be enough rival players around to shoot it in.

The only time you concede an edge to the other club is on their power play. You can't be overly aggressive when killing a penalty. If you take a man out, all you're doing is cutting the play from four on five to three on four—and four on five is easier to defend. The trick is to force the issue but not get caught out of position, and this takes experience.

You've got to keep mobile. The idea of the power play is to gain possession of the puck in the attacking zone, then pass it around until you can hit the open man. To defense this, you set up in a standard box formation with your defensemen back near the net and your two forwards halfway to the points. Most clubs will set up their power play with two men at the points and two more in the corners, with the extra man in the slot. As they move the puck back and forth between the points, into the corners and behind the net, the defensive box shifts with the

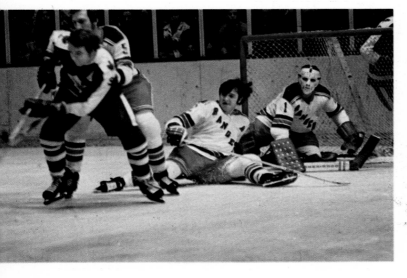

Imlach believes in aggressiveness. "I'm not waiting for you to make a move so I can counter," he says. *Above:* Brad Park goes down to make a stop, forcing Norm Ullman to scurry after the puck. *Opposite:* Bob Plager comes over blue line to check Dennis Hextall.

play. Basically, you're just trying to keep the puck outside the perimeter of the box. But if they get the puck to the man in the slot, one of the wingmen has to come back and take him.

For example, if the puck comes out of the southeast corner, the wingman from the northwest corner collapses on the guy in the slot. This obviously leaves the point man open, but what you're always trying to do is to leave him the worst shot possible. It's better to have someone shooting from 50 feet away than from 25. The more you can force the other team to pass the puck around, the more time they'll use up. There's also a chance that they'll blow a pass and enable you to jump in there and clear the puck.

Of course, you can try to bottle them up in their own end before they get started, but again, this depends on your personnel. Even against those great Montreal power plays with Beliveau and Boom Boom Geoffrion and Dickie Moore and Doug Harvey, I wasn't afraid to send Keon in there immediately. Keon was a tireless skater, smooth and fast enough to get back on defense if they did move the puck out on him. Basically, there are two ways of approaching a power play before it reaches your end, and the one you use depends upon your players.

For example, when they stop behind their net, you can have your man—say Keon—pull up in front with your second man—in our case it was usually George Armstrong—circling behind him in a kind of I-formation. As their man starts out, Keon picks him up and tries to force him toward the boards, making sure he doesn't cut back across the flow of play. He can't get the puck over to the other side of the ice, so he's got to keep moving into the boards. If he tries to pass the puck ahead, Armstrong will either intercept or pick up the man who gets it. If they stop and go back behind the net, naturally you will set up in front and start all over again.

In some cases I used this method, which was made popular by Eddie Shore in Springfield, but usually I went with the second method, because, as I've said, you use what fits your players. Because we had solid skaters in guys like Keon and Kelly and checkers like Armstrong and Bob Pulford, I might have sent two men in on left and right wing. They would crisscross in front of the net and come back with the play. But we also had these great defensemen, so occasionally I'd just let the other club go ahead and bang their heads against the wall. We'd pick up their wings and let them bring the puck to

our blue line, where our defensemen would stand up (challenge the puck carrier) and force them to shoot it in. Our guys were so good at coming up with the puck in our own end, or else freezing it along the boards and then winning the face-off, that this method seemed to fit us best. The advantage of having Keon and Armstrong and Pulford and Ron Stewart was that I could operate either way. I've used both methods here in Buffalo, but we haven't had the skaters to go in and forecheck that well. We've usually just had our wings come back and make them shoot it in.

When you have the power play, you have to try to get control of the puck in their end of the rink. You either shoot it in and chase it, trying to force a stoppage of play, or carry it in and set up when all your players get inside their zone. As always, how you play it depends upon your personnel.

During the early part of the 1971–72 season,

Buffalo probably scored more goals on the power play than anyone else in the league, because we had Gil Perreault and Rick Martin. Perreault (who is going to be one of the great players in the league someday) can swoop into their end on the right side and set up when everyone gets inside the blue line. Martin scored 44 goals in his first year. Boston does the same thing with Orr and Esposito. Both of them can carry the puck and, once they're in your zone, there's no guarantee that they're going to stop and wait for everyone else. They may just keep going in on your goal crease.

If you make them stop, they will set up with men at the points and in the corners and one guy, usually Esposito, in the slot. On the power play, the slot man is the one you want to get the puck. If you defense by converging on the slot man, they'll send the puck back to the points, where Orr and Fred Stanfield have

"You can't wait on a team or they'll kill you." *Opposite:* Harry Howell attacks Garry Unger. *Left:* John Bucyk plays aggressively against Jean Ratelle.

"Basically, my strategy is to keep moving." In motion are St. Louis's Barclay Plager and Minnesota's Barry Gibbs *(left)*, Terry O'Reilly and Alex Delvecchio *(above)*.

the big shots. With everybody jamming up in front of the net, the goaltender hasn't got much chance of seeing the puck. If somebody like Orr or Bobby Hull is firing it, the puck is moving so fast that sometimes you're not going to stop it even if you do see it. Regardless of what you do, teams like Boston are going to score a lot of goals on the power play, and it doesn't matter whether they're shooting from close in or far out.

Boston also has wings Ken Hodge and Wayne Cashman—big, tough guys who can go into the corners and behind the net and come up with the puck. With players like that, it's to their advantage to shoot the puck in. The Bruins, then, can beat you in a variety of ways.

Trying to anticipate how they're going to bring it in is a threat in itself. Here comes Esposito with the puck. He can't carry it in, so he throws it into the corner. Cashman or Hodge barrels in after it, and Esposito follows the play. You know that Hodge or

Cashman is going to take one defenseman out of the play. The puck is probably loose, and here comes Esposito to grab it. Or maybe Phil just ties up the other defenseman that might be there and slaps the puck around the boards to the point. Bingo. Esposito disengages and moves into the slot. Hull and Stan Mikita were the same way with Chicago. When one of them was on the point, someone would just wheel that puck around the boards to him, and sometimes I was afraid to watch, because I knew how either of them could fire that puck.

If we were at even strength against Chicago, I would usually have Keon pick up Hull or Mikita as he came out from behind their net. I'd have him stay with Hull or Mikita all the way, because it's better to have anyone else carrying the puck toward your goal than either of them. It's like baseball, where you're never supposed to let a .350 hitter beat you if you can avoid it. Take your chances on the .250 hitter. If you kill off a great team's power play, it can give your club a

great emotional lift and maybe even turn the whole hockey game around.

I'm always looking for the edge, regardless of how slight it might be. For instance, in Toronto, when we were killing a penalty, I always had the defenseman take the face-off in our zone. It was different from everyone else's way, but I figured that the defenseman's natural position was close to the net. His job was to tie up the man he faced off with, and if the puck went out toward the blue line, both wingmen would then be free to cover the points, which were their natural positions. Since the defenseman couldn't go out there, he was better off taking the face-off. Naturally, they changed the rule on me. Now you can't interfere with a man on the face-off. The rule was introduced when we were winning all those Stanley Cups, and I argued against it strenuously. You've got to check people, and my defenseman's got just as much right to tie up a man in the face-off circle as he does in front of the net.

It seems that whenever you're successful, they legislate against you. They can't beat you on the ice, so they try to beat you with the rule book. When Montreal had that great power play in the fifties, one penalty could kill you. Boston was leading the Canadiens, 2–0, and got simultaneous minor penalties. Well, before those guys got out of the box, the score was

3–2, Montreal. Game over. The next year, they ruled that as soon as one goal was scored on the power play, the penalized team was returned to equal strength.

When Carl Brewer was with the Maple Leafs, he would cut the palms out of his gloves, so that when somebody tried to go around him, he could grab the man, and all the referee could see were the fingers of Brewer's glove lying flat. So they introduced a rule making it illegal to cut out the palms of your gloves.

Soon after Hull and Mikita invented the curved stick, legislation outlawed sticks with more than a one-inch curvature in the blade. That rule was probably justified. Sooner or later, a goalie was going to get killed.

It's not easy to stay on top in this league. The top spot seems to go in cycles. Detroit had great teams in the early and mid-fifties. Then the Canadiens took over. It was Toronto in the early sixties. The Canadiens came back for a while, and then Boston got Orr, and now they're in the driver's seat.

As both a coach and general manager in Toronto, I was criticized for keeping my veterans around after they had won their third straight Stanley Cup in 1964. And I admit I probably carried this loyalty to my players to extremes. But I also think that by keeping my veterans, I got us a Stanley Cup in 1967 that we

otherwise wouldn't have won. I believed then, and I still believe, that the people who put you on top should stay around to enjoy the view.

If Buffalo should win the Stanley Cup, however, I don't know that I would stand pat the way I did with Toronto. Those Leafs—Horton, Stanley, Baun, Armstrong, Kelly, Dickie Duff—were great people. And how can I forget Johnny Bower? The toughest job I've had in the hockey business was telling some of those guys that they were finished. What you're saying is that you can't use them anymore, and that's a damn hard thing to say. Being part of the game doesn't make it any easier.

I remember a game in the Stanley Cup finals against Montreal in Toronto in 1967. With less than a minute to go, we were leading, 2–1. There was a face-off in our end, so I put all the old men out there —Horton, Stanley, Kelly, Armstrong, Pulford. Stanley shoveled the face-off to Kelly behind him. Kelly got the puck up to Armstrong, who went down and scored into the empty net. That was the game and the Cup. A lot of people thought that I was being sentimental, putting those guys out there, but I went with the guys I thought could do the job. They were veterans. They were the least likely to make a mistake. When you get down to that stage of the game, you're not going to be sentimental—although I admit it's kind of nice now to look back and remember who was out there in the end.

Obviously, a coach's relationship with his players

Trying to gain control of the puck are Bobby Orr *(left)*, Flames' Morris Stefaniw and Sabres' Rick Martin *(below)*. Against Orr, says Imlach, there is no strategy.

is extremely important. Very seldom would I berate a player in front of the entire team. Not over once a year would I do something like that, and then only if I had to. I always tried to talk to the players as a team, so that when I made certain general remarks, the guy in question knew that I was talking about him. Embarrassing him in front of the entire club wasn't necessary.

People are all different. If you go to the paper mill on Monday morning and press the button, the machine will go on. It will run for eight hours. Press the button and it goes off. Same thing Tuesday and every other day of the week. But players aren't machines. They have no buttons. When a guy gets up in the morning, he doesn't feel the same as he did

yesterday morning. So you treat players according to their individual personalities, although you try not to make it look that way. You run the club as a unit, but you don't overlook a player's personality and his attitudes.

I was criticized for the way I handled Frank Mahovlich and a few of the other stars. But Mahovlich was harnessed to the team. He couldn't just play any way he wanted. He had to play according to the system. Offensively he could do anything he liked, but on defense he had certain responsibilities. That he was a star didn't mean that he was exempt from certain things.

It's a little different here in Buffalo, where we're trying to build a new hockey club. We're trying to

Above: A convenient crack in the wall and a blowtorch are modern stick-curving methods. *Opposite:*
Two-on-one break with the wing keeping the puck himself.

build a clientele, trying to establish a star. Perreault is a star, and there used to be things he didn't have to do. We didn't get on his back because he didn't check. But now we will, and do. After all, he is a member of the team. Everyone is in the same boat. I know that sounds corny, but that's the only attitude with which you're going to win consistently. I learned a lot from watching the original six expansion teams approach their games with Toronto. Those that succeeded played a strict defensive game. They just picked up their wings and laid back and hoped for a break. They took no chances offensively. In Buffalo we decided upon the opposite approach. Although I'm a defensive coach, I recognize the dangers of being too defensive-minded. For one thing, you're never going to improve your offense. So although we instituted the defensive system I've been talking about, we have also encouraged our skaters to go out and score goals. There's no way you'll see us going into a shell with scorers like Perreault and Martin around.

But through it all, you've got to maintain that team feeling of being in the thing together. Sometimes it isn't easy, because, as I said, everybody's different. I'm not easy to live with, or at least I wasn't before I had my heart attack. I'm abrasive, and I'm a perfectionist. I'm a stubborn SOB. I want to win. As a perfectionist, I'm prepared to put in all kinds of time, and I expect my players to do the same. I've poured my guts into this game, and it's ruined my health. A perfectionist thinks you can be better than you are. I don't care how fast you skate, you can always skate a little faster. I don't care how hard you hit somebody, you can always hit a little harder. I believe this. The human body can always do better if you force it. If you don't force it, you'll never know. You've got to take that extra step.

You may have better players, but if my players are in better shape, we're going to win. We'll be able to go further and last longer. Some coaches say that to practice more than 30 minutes will only tire out your players. Well, I've always said a miler doesn't prepare to run a mile by running 400 yards a day. He runs 8, 10, 15 miles. I don't think you can go full speed for 30 minutes in a hockey game if you have only practiced for 30 minutes. If you're going to go 30, you should practice 90. Even in March. I recognize the fact that you can overtrain and get let down. But over the course of the season, everybody has a letdown, so let's have ours early and be ready when the play-offs come around. Some guys say they're

going to pace themselves. To me, that's ridiculous. In this game, the only way you're going to be a winner is to drive all the way.

The Russian players demonstrated this better than anything I could have said. I used to get all kinds of criticism because I took my players directly to practice from the train or plane. No matter what, they were going to be on that ice—and not for one and a half hours but for two and a half. Nobody's loafing. Everybody's working. And isn't that where the Russians are? As far as I'm concerned, the Russians drew a red line under my philosophy. Our guys weren't ready to play them in Canada, but they were ready by the time they got to Russia. That, and a lot of desire, paid off. There's no easy way.

A coach must convince his players to perform. Simply that I believe you should perform doesn't mean you will; I've got to get my ideas across to you. This is the toughest part of coaching. Being physically prepared is only half the battle. The other half is

being mentally ready. The secret to success is a combination of instruction and salesmanship. When the coach goes into that locker room, half the time he's just doing a salesman's job, selling the game to the players. You use any gimmick you can come up with. Once, in that first year when we won the Stanley Cup, I sent out for $2,500—the winner's share for the semifinals—in 25 packs of 100 singles. While the guys were out warming up for the game, I stacked the money in the middle of the dressing room. When they came back in, they stood gawking at that pile, and I said, "Now look, that's your money. Don't let the other guy put his hand in your pocket." They went out and won the game.

Another time, we were going into Montreal for a big game. I went out and bought up a bunch of books on the power of positive thinking. I endorsed them and said, "Here, this is how you do it," as I gave them to my players. "Read it. Believe it." Again they won. This sounds corny, but a lot depends on

psyching your players up. Anything you can do to get them up for a game, you do.

Let's assume that you've got these two players. One is the greatest player in the world and knows it, but he's 20 pounds overweight. The other is a guy who's in fantastic shape, but doesn't have the desire —can't be bothered. One's as bad as the other. Neither will ever be a winner. What you've got to have is a mixture of desire and conditioning. Put both of them together, and believe me, you're in business. I've had players like that. They were winners.

As a guy gets older, he becomes less dedicated. Not only does he get a step slower, he also loses his desire to mix it up. He becomes more lover than fighter. This happens to everybody. It's human nature. A coach just has to realize it. When you get him as a kid, he'll go through a brick wall for you, but after he's played for seven or eight years, he's not so apt to go through that wall. He may have gotten married. His wife may tell him not to get hurt. Maybe she doesn't like fighting, and subconsciously he's worried about that. She says, "Look, don't make a fool out of me; I'm sitting up there in the stands. Don't fight." Well, he's got to live with her a lot longer than he's got to live with me. All these things, of course, enter into running a hockey club. Sometimes they'll keep you up at night, sometimes a lot of nights.

I take pride in the fact that I won with old guys everybody else said were all washed up. By pushing them that extra mile, I gave a lot of them four or five more years. Hell, Armstrong came out of retirement four times to play for me. Baun and Horton are still playing. Horton's 42 years old, and I'm tickled just to have him with us.

Of course, there are always exceptions. In 1964 I traded to get Andy Bathgate from New York. I had been trying to get him for two years, and when I finally did, it was because New York was convinced he was finished. I knew he was near the end, but I didn't think we could win the Cup without him. Well, we won the Cup that year, and the summer after that, Andy really blasted me in the newspapers. He said that there was a limit to what players could take and that I pushed players beyond that limit. I don't deny that. The job of a coach is to get as much as possible out of his players.

Of course, being stubborn isn't exactly the nicest personality trait to have. Still, there are times when it comes in handy. You don't quit. You don't concede to anybody. Nothing's going to beat you. I recognize

Opposite: Vic Hadfield chases the puck in deep. Unless a team is desperate to score, one man goes after the puck while two men stay out, ready either to shoot or to backcheck. *Above:* Pat Stapleton leads the attack against Minnesota while Bob Nevin defends.

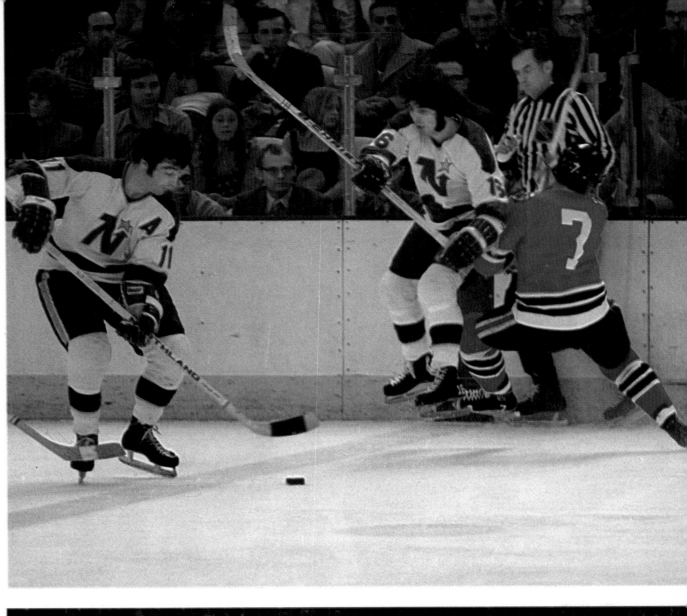

the pitfalls of it, but nevertheless, that's the way I am.

Very rarely would I go into the dressing room right after a period was over unless I was really mad and the team was playing horribly. That happens sometimes, though. Then you storm into that room and lay it on the line and storm out. But usually I'd go and watch the period on the video tape machine, see how the goals were scored and who was in or out of position. All the time, though, I'd be looking for a theme. A hockey game is mistakes, and you could spend the whole rest period telling your club what it did wrong. Then they don't get any rest, or they don't pay any attention to you. You're kind of like a nagging wife. So what I would do was to wait until a few minutes before it was time to return to the ice, and then I'd go in and tell them that they weren't shooting the puck or that they weren't skating or backchecking. Something basic. Then, after we went out, maybe I would get a guy on the bench and point out specifically what he had done wrong and what he should do to correct it.

When you have coached for a long time, you find yourself saying the same things over and over. In Toronto there were players who had been around for 10 years who would see me coming out into the room and think, here comes lecture number 12 again. Or number 15. Or number 18. I probably could have taped some of those spiels and run them on the video tape machine and saved myself a lot of breath. But at the same time, if something's wrong, it has to be talked about. Most of the things that go wrong in a hockey game aren't particularly complex; lots of them are just the result of carelessness or fatigue or just plain laziness. It's up to the coach to bring them up.

By far the worst thing that can happen out there is for your club to start running around, especially in their own end. As I've said, on offense my players can more or less free-lance out there, taking advantage of the other club's weaknesses or position at the exchange of the puck. But on defense they've got certain men to pick up, places to be at a given time. When they're running around, they aren't in position. They're not organized. They start following the puck around, not their checks. It starts when one guy doesn't do his job. The next guy tries to help him out, but he can't cover two men, and the situation just gets worse. Pretty soon you've got two or three players trying to do the same job and none of them doing it. If you don't get them straightened out fast, the puck winds up in your net.

Face-offs in your own end of the rink are critical. You have a 50–50 chance of getting the puck, but if you lose it and one of your players is out of position, the other team will get a good shot on your net. What you always try to do is to keep a man between the puck and the net. The boss man out there is the guy who takes the face-off for us; he will not go into that circle until everyone's in position and knows exactly who to cover. Essentially, you play the opponents man for man; the way they set up fairly well dictates how you will line up.

Suppose that the face-off is in our zone, to the left of the goaltender *(below)*. Many clubs like to line up with their centerman taking the draw, a wingman to his left at the rim of the face-off circle, another wingman in the slot and both defensemen at the points. In this case, we'll probably have our centerman take the draw. Then we'll have three men in a line—both wings on the outside and a defenseman in the middle. They set up from the rim of the face-off circle, and the other defenseman is behind our centerman. The puck is dropped. Immediately, both my wingmen start out to cover the point men. The defenseman ties up their wing at the rim of the circle, and my centerman, although he can't interfere with their centerman, detains him as best he can. I mean, if their centerman scores a goal, Heaven help the guy who faced off with him, because *that's his man!*

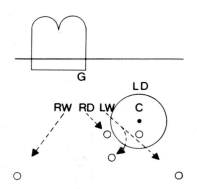

The only way we can get hurt here is by their man in the slot. But even here, my wingman is busting out in the direction of the right point, and if he sees the puck go to the man in the slot, he's still got a chance to pick him up.

Sometimes the other club will line up straight across, with their center taking the face-off, his wings on either side at the rim of the circle and the defensemen at the points. What they have done, essentially,

Top: Pit Martin stops Jude Drouin, who still manages to get off a pass to breaking teammate Jean-Paul Parisé. *Bottom:* Delvecchio draws two Bruins before passing to flying Alan Karlander.

is to take the man out of the slot and put him along the right boards *(below)*. Fine. We put a man there too. If the puck goes to the right point *(right)*, our wingman along the boards still has to go out and force the play. The defenseman behind our centerman then becomes responsible for their wing along the boards. He doesn't exactly take him, but he makes sure he stays between that winger and the net. My center takes their center, my other defenseman takes their wing at the rim of the circle and my other wing goes

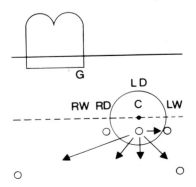

out to cover the left point. As you can see, it always comes down to five men on five. Everybody should be —everybody had *better* be—covered.

There are only so many variations that can develop from that circle. There are 180 degrees for you, 180 for them. If the puck is drawn into your 180, fine. You're organized, and you know how you're supposed to come out with it. If they win the draw, there are still only so many things that can happen, and when you've practiced this situation enough, none of them

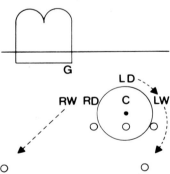

Preceding pages: Lou Angotti flies over goalie Dryden in unsuccessful attempt to score. *Above:* Rangers Seiling, DeMarco, Irvine. *Opposite:* Ratelle tries to draw puck back against Kings' Vic Venasky.

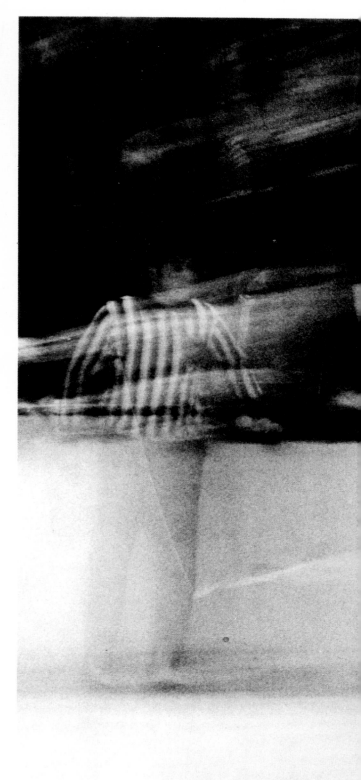

Two of Imlach's tenets: aggressiveness *(left)* and movement *(below)*. "As soon as you get the puck, turn on the offense. When you lose it, switch immediately to defense."

should surprise you. The only guy who can really hurt you is that man in the slot, especially if he's got a shot like Bobby Hull's. Goals are going to be scored from there; you realize that. You also realize that the law of averages says they're not always going to get the puck to that guy, and even when they do you've still got that defenseman between him and the net. When they've got a guy like Hull sitting there, just waiting to blast it, it's up to your centerman to make sure that they don't drag the puck to him. You don't care where it's drawn, just so it doesn't go to Hull. What you're hoping is that you can tie up the play long enough for the defenseman to jump in there— he's got his reach and a stick length working for him —and either break up the play or pick up the puck himself.

To be honest, I don't like to line up straight across on offense when the face-off is in their end. I like to put a man in the slot—someone like Rick Martin—who can really shoot. Perreault wins the draw and gets it to Martin in the slot. Not a bad piece of strategy.

We always try to play things right. There's no sense in taking unnecessary chances. I may gamble $20 or so on a horse race once in a while, but I'll never gamble in a hockey game unless I have to. I'm always looking for an edge, but I'll never give

anything away. For example, we say as little about our injuries as possible—and so do most other clubs —because you can run at a guy who's injured. They say that everything's fair in love and war, and as far as I'm concerned, this is war. If I know you've got a bad arm, I'm going to take a stick to it. If I know you've got a bad ankle, I'm going to try and get at it. And the sooner the better. If you can't play because you're hurt, that's tough. But if I don't know you're hurt, I might not play you the same way.

Gordie Howe has played with a broken thumb and a broken rib; Bobby Baun once played for me on a broken ankle; lots of guys play all the time with something broken or hurting pretty bad. That's the name of this game. One year that we won the Stanley Cup, we had guys being shot all the time. Bob Pulford's shoulder was hurting him pretty bad, and he was getting it frozen for every game. But nobody knew he was hurt, and nobody knew he was being shot. We had three guys getting shot during those play-offs, and you can't tell me that if the other clubs had known they were in trouble, they wouldn't have taken some extra runs. After everything was over, though, it came out about our guys getting shot, and one fan even sent a letter to the Minister of Justice, complaining that I was being inhumane to hockey players. Nonsense! I was just making them available for play.

On my club, the doors are never opened to the newspapermen until after the players have been checked over, treated, unwrapped and unstrapped. And nobody is allowed in the room before a game. You get a lot of cooperation from hockey players on this policy.

Among other things, I've been accused of being too conservative; it has been charged that my teams in Toronto were willing to go out, get a one-goal lead and sit on it all night if they could. I don't think we were as defensive-minded as all that, but we did sit on leads. Why not? The object of the game is to win. And the way you sit on a lead is to play it the same way you always do, only better. You don't take the chance of getting trapped in their end. You're not going to gamble for another goal. Otherwise, you may commit three men on a rush, not score and allow the other team a three-on-two break.

I remember the game in Montreal, the seventh game of the Stanley Cup semifinals in 1964, the year we won our third Cup in a row. We were winning, 2–1, in the third period. I wanted my guys to play defensively, but they wouldn't. I've never seen anything like it in my life. Three Canadiens would be on a rush, but they wouldn't score. Bower was sensational for us that night. Suddenly we got a three-man break. We were winning, 2–1, but our guys went in to

104

Above: The all-important face-off. For the Rangers it's Stemkowski on the draw, Irvine (27) to his side and MacGregor on the rim of the circle. *Left:* Half the Vancouver team tries to block the shot.

Backchecking is vital. Here, Goalie Villemure has moved out to block an angle shot, but the puck has come to Seal Craig Patrick. Defensemen Park and Rolfe are out of position, and forward Irvine must stop the shot.

Conflicting styles of defense: Vancouver defenseman Barry Wilkins (above) goes down to the ice to block puck, while Seal Croteau (opposite) goes down to block man.

try to score, and their goaltender was as great as Bower. Then they came back, three on two. It went back and forth like that, and I was standing behind the bench and saying, "Geez, will you guys quit? One goal is enough!" But I couldn't stop the momentum of the game. The Canadiens were pulling out all stops to tie, and since we'd always told our guys to exploit what they could, they'd try to capitalize on three men trapped in our zone. And then we would get caught. And then they would come back. It went back and forth like this for about 10 minutes, until Keon finally scored his third goal into an empty net, and we won the game. I don't think I've ever seen a more exciting 10 minutes of hockey in my life, but while it was great hockey for the fans, it was all wrong for the coach.

You don't take chances when you're ahead. If the puck comes free in the corner, your second guy in doesn't even go for it. Even if there's better than a 50–50 chance of getting it, he just turns and comes back with his check. The first guy in is checking the opposition. If they make a bad pass and he comes up with the puck, he just gives it over to the second guy. You rag it as much as you can. When they come after you, you just throw it back into their end and let them start all over again. Let them break their backs. You've got the edge.

If we're behind, say, 2–1, we're not going to play games until there's only six or seven minutes to go. We'll try to put more pressure on them, force them into mistakes and play a little harder, but we won't take any wild chances. We won't take a defenseman off and put an extra forward out there. After all, one goal for us, and it's a brand new hockey game.

With five minutes to go, behind by one goal in a game I need desperately, I might wait until we get a face-off in their end and put my power play out there. Then time is definitely working in their favor, and we've got to really start shooting for that tying goal. If it gets down to a minute or a minute and a half, we'll probably pull our goaltender. If we're down by two goals, we naturally have to start looking for something a little earlier. But even if we get a goal with three minutes to go, we're still only down by one, and now we've got a chance to tie it up. We just can't pull out all stops too soon.

If we're playing one man in and one out, I may wait until there are two minutes to go—when I'm down by two goals—and then it's two men in and one out.

We go in and get the bloody puck and forget about backchecking. But so much depends upon your personnel. When you haven't got super players, you have to wait for the other club to make the mistakes, because you haven't the ability to take the puck from them on your own. You keep on backchecking and hope that they'll get goal-hungry. That happens a lot, and you only have to catch them once.

There are times when everything you're trying to do goes wrong. Then you've got to do something to shake everybody up. I've pulled the goaltender in the first period when I was down, 4–0, mostly to change the game and force a psychological reversal in my players. What's the difference between 4–0 and 5–0? It's as if you're telling your guys and the crowd, "Look: I want to win this hockey game. You may not

want to, but I do." I've also put six forwards out there. Sometimes it shocks everybody so much that something happens. Hell, being down 4–0 at the end of the first period isn't the end of the world. We've come back to win many games in my career after being down that much that early. You simply go to an approach that is more psychological than strategical.

In a close game, when you're tied or the difference is a goal either way, the heat is really on the coach. I'm thinking about who I'm going to have ready for the last shift on the ice five minutes before the game is over. I've got to start juggling lines so that the people I think can do the job are going to become available with a minute or a minute and a half to go. They will have to be fresh at that time. I might double shift a line to set this up, and all the

time I'm watching what the other coach is doing with his players. If he starts to put his best out there with three minutes to go, well, I'll have to counter with my best checkers at the same time. I just hope that my team is in better shape than his, so that I can come back with those guys if I have to. I certainly can't leave them out there for three minutes. I have to try to blunt the other club for a minute, come back with another line, then come back with my best checkers again. If we're ahead, I know damn well he's going to go with his best scorers on the ice in the last minute, with his goaltender out. If I'm down by the goal, I'm going to use my big scorers two out of the last three minutes. That's when you find out who's in shape and who's not.

If I'm ahead late in a close game, I'll try to slow things down. I'll take my time putting my players on the ice. I'll change them one at a time. I'll call a player over to talk to me. It may take five minutes to play the last two minutes. All the time, my big guys are getting the rest they need.

Some goaltenders, the late Terry Sawchuck for one, were particularly adept at finding a broken piece of tape or a loose strap or a skate that needed repair. What you're trying to do, of course, is to stop the momentum of the opposing players. Once they get that momentum, they're all over you. Maybe they're at home and their crowd is spurring them on, forcing them to play over their heads. You want to stop it, keep from letting that momentum overpower you.

I remember a play-off game in Chicago in 1962.

Above: Dennis Hull has turned the defense but comes in too tight, allowing Dryden to poke away the puck. *Right:* Punch Imlach outlines a magnetic strategy.

The muscle, the reach and the shot. *Above:* Ken Hodge wards off trouble with one hand while maintaining stick control with the other. *Opposite top:* Jean Ratelle covers 10 feet of ice with balance and reach. *Opposite bottom:* Islander Tom Miller fires a slapper.

It was the third period, score tied at zero. The Hawks were coming. They were really playing well. All of a sudden, they scored with 10 minutes left in the game. I want to tell you, 20,000 people went out of their heads. They threw so much stuff on the ice that it took 10 minutes to clean it up. In that 10 minutes, hell, the Hawks lost all their momentum. We scored two goals and won the game, 2–1. If it's close and your opponents are putting on any pressure at all, you're going to make it tougher on them if you slow things down. They're itching to get at you, but you're going to make them wait. If their crowd is throwing stuff on the ice, that's great.

So late in the game, I'll do anything I can to slow it up, and I know my players will do the same. They'll hold the puck against the boards. They'll cause a lot of stoppages, not only to give them the rest they need but also to allow me to make any changes I may want. If the puck goes into their end of the rink, there's only one thing my guys want to do—tie it up. Same thing in our end. There's no way, if the puck's going into our end, that my guys will take a chance on a bad pass. They're going to tie up the puck. We'll all get organized for the face-off and then take it from there. We don't want a face-off in our end. But, confident that we know what we're going to do, I would prefer to play it that way. I mean, I've seen clubs of mine with 30 seconds left to go get as many as five face-offs in our end of the rink. But as I see it, five face-offs and the game is over. We'll know what we're going to do on every one of those face-offs. I don't care if it takes 20 face-offs in the last 30 seconds. The other club is not going to score that goal.

You can cover as many points as you want on strategy, but it all comes down to one thing: Your club has to work as a team. Your players all help each other. Look at all your great teams, regardless of the sport; ask the players about it, and they'll say they're all in it together and that they feel for one another. No one is alone out there. Look at Bobby Orr, one of the greatest players ever. When he's with the writers, he's always talking team, team, team. It's the same thing with Howe, Beliveau, all the great ones. That's the way I always tried to work it with the Leafs, and that's the way we're handling it here in Buffalo. I tell the players when we start training camp, before we go on the ice, "You're all my friends. We're going to have our problems, and you're not always going to play as well as I want you to play. Maybe you're going to step out of line and I'm going to have to censure you. Maybe

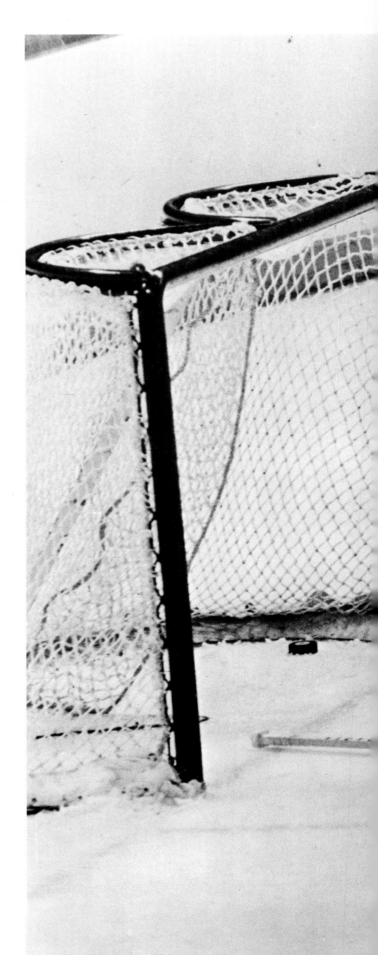

fine you. But at the end of the hockey season, as far as I'm concerned, you're still my friends."

Some people can't accept that kind of talk. Maybe they don't believe it, or think you're trying to take advantage of them. But I mean it. Regardless of what has gone on during the season, there's no hard feelings. That's honestly the way I am.

I've got a good man behind the bench—Joe Crozier. (He's there because, with my bad heart, I'm not.) And that's where games are won. General manager sounds important, but in my book, if you can be a good bank clerk, you can be a good general manager. You have to run the club where it counts—on the ice. That's what I love to do. I guess that, were it not for my heart attack, I never would have quit the damn job. But there are certain things in life a man has to face, and that is one of mine. At this particular time, I would say that there is no way I will ever take the chance of returning to coaching. But that's not to say that I won't miss it. You don't give 25 years of your life to something and not miss it.

Right: Mike Murphy, one-on-one, successfully completes scoring play. *Above:* Buffalo coach Crozier sets to send in "The French Connection."

4 The Million-dollar Power Play

JAMES D. NORRIS

(For payment in full for player
Frank Mahovlich)

PAY TO THE
ORDER OF Toronto Maple L

One Million Dollars ------

TO

THE FIRST NATIONAL BA

OF CHICAGO

CHICAGO, ILL.

NO. **864**

$$\frac{2-1}{710}$$

ICAGO ,ILL. **October 6** 19 **62**

Hockey Club $ **1,000,000.00**

nadian Funds)------ **DOLLARS**

James D. Norris

They come from all over Canada, hockey's general managers. They come from big towns like Montreal and Toronto and little ones like North Battleford and South Porcupine. They come in all shapes and sizes and from all kinds of backgrounds. One used to drive a milk truck in Oshawa. Another peddled sound equipment in Quebec. Another promoted theater attractions in Pittsburgh and another was in the egg business in upstate New York.

Depending on the club he works for, as well as his personal blend of conviction and con, the hockey GM is a somebody or a nobody; a veritable dictator with the future of a multimillion-dollar franchise in his hands or a front man for an owner determined to pull the strings. But always, his is a life of 20-hour days and sleepless nights, of wheeling and dealing and backdoor maneuvering. The interleague draft, the intraleague draft. Late scores from the coast, the shot that hit the post. A quick trip into deepest Canada to check out a scout's assertion that he has, indeed, found the next Bobby Orr.

Without someone who can cut it in the smoke-filled rooms of the National Hockey League, a team stands little chance of a division championship or a Stanley Cup. In Boston during the late twenties and thirties, it was Art Ross who put the Bruins on top. In New York, it was Lester Patrick. Conn Smythe not only built a dynasty in Toronto—he built Maple Leaf Gardens during the Depression. From the mid-forties and into the sixties, it was Montreal's Frank Selke and Detroit's Jack Adams producing talent that dominated the league as it had never been dominated before.

Today, the unchallenged master of the smoke-filled room is a short, scruffy fellow in Montreal named Sam Pollock, who assumed command of the Canadiens when Selke retired. Pollock is also known around the NHL as "The Godfather." He makes deals that lesser teams can't refuse. "Sam's got about nine top draft choices that he just keeps revolving into the Canadiens every year," says Punch Imlach, Buffalo's general manager. "Whenever a club goes to him for help he says, 'Look. I've got a real good hockey player here. Two real good hockey players. They can help you right now. You want them? Fine. Give me your number one draft choice three years from now.' "

"Some think Sam is the all-time general manager and others say he inherited the talent from Selke," says Bill Torrey of the New York Islanders. "But others have had the talent and kicked it away. I personally think Sam's about as sharp as they come. Whenever I come out of his office, I make it a point to glance in the mirror and check myself front and back."

Pollock is an expert at spotting trends. He is constantly submitting legislation to the NHL's Board of Governors and getting it passed. When some of the new rules ultimately turn out to benefit the Canadiens more than anyone else, there is naturally a feeling among his rivals that they have been outslicked. "Sam's first love was baseball," says NHL president Clarence Campbell, who has observed Pollock in action for years. "I don't know if he studied Branch Rickey or not, but Sam's very much like him. All of Rickey's rivals feared him because they felt he would get them sooner or later. I think the same feeling exists with regard to doing business with Mr. Pollock."

Of course, Pollock scoffs at such suggestions. "Look," he says, "the longer you're in this business, the more contacts you acquire. This is extremely valuable. There's no way you can have one of your people in every area all the time, so you have to depend on people who, through the years, may have become friendly toward you or your organization. I've been fortunate in this regard. Without the contacts I've made through the years, I'm nothing."

Sam Pollock, now 48, is not a pretentious man. In fact, nursing a Scotch and soda in a hotel suite during last year's Stanley Cup play-offs, the only thing that distinguished Pollock from the newspapermen around him was his rumpled blue blazer with the Montreal Canadiens' emblem on the breast pocket. Sam's home life means a great deal to him, and he hates to fly so much that he twice drove to Minnesota and back, 1,200 miles, to watch the 1971 play-off finals between his club and the North Stars.

Clarence Campbell says that Pollock epitomizes the type of hockey man known in Canada as a "snowbanker," or an individual who learned his hockey the hard way and expects everyone else to do the same.

"A snowbanker," Campbell explains, "has an inherent distrust of anyone who didn't come up the way he did. He is a man who, because he didn't possess the potential to make the pros, gravitated to the operation of kids' leagues and minor league clubs. At a time when competition was at its peak, he earned his spurs. He shoveled snow off the outdoor rinks so that his team could play. He learned how to promote, spend, save, influence and trade. He taught himself

everything there was to the game, from the recruitment of players and promoting the team to learning the rules and the bylaws to the letter.

"It became an attitude, a philosophy of hard work, that still holds true today in men like Pollock and Scotty Bowman and Tommy Ivan and, to a degree, Cliff Fletcher in Atlanta. However, because of his sales experience, Fletcher is smoother, more public-relations conscious. Frank Selke was just like that. He surrounded himself with men who were just like he was—keen, cunning, distrustful of others."

Over the years, Campbell says, the fundamental knowledge of such men has proven generally sounder than that of their contemporaries. "In their hard, competitive backgrounds, it was tested by crisis, both team and personal. They seem to have more answers at more levels. And they're all business. Whereas a man like Milt Schmidt, who was a player himself, might have difficulty trading a player because of the emotional upheaval involved, the Pollocks and the Bowmans and the Ivans regard such a move as nothing more than a transfer of contracts, of sheets of paper, of documents spelling out services to be provided."

"For the most part this is a pretty cold-blooded business," agrees Tommy Ivan, general manager of the Chicago Black Hawks. "You just can't let sentiment or emotion enter into your decisions."

A dapper little man who coached the Detroit Red Wings through most of their glory years, Ivan has been the Chicago GM for 16 years. He is from the old school. He is a tough bargainer. He is crafty and cautious. "I'm also extremely fortunate to have been able to work for essentially the same people for twenty-five years. In Detroit it was Pop Norris—James Norris, Senior—and over here it was his son, Jim, and Arthur Wirtz. I became very close to these people."

Ivan, who is 62 years old, gazed around his office in Chicago Stadium. There were thick, rose-colored carpeting on the floor and framed photographs of past teams and old friends on the paneled walls. "I've also been very fortunate to have been where there were some pretty good hockey players. As a coach in Detroit I had guys like Howe and Lindsay and Kelly and Sawchuck, and here in Chicago you could start the list with Hull and Mikita."

In 1954, the Chicago Black Hawks were in deep trouble. They were the doormats of the league—in six of the last eight seasons they had finished in last place. Fewer than 4,000 people were turning out for games in cavernous Chicago Stadium, and the franchise appeared doomed financially. But Jim Norris and Arthur Wirtz had just purchased the club. Norris, who had made his name in the boxing and race-horse businesses, once said that he could lay his hands on $300 million if he had to, and Wirtz's wealth, accumulated through extensive real estate, banking and hotel interests, was almost as great. "Both men went into Chicago with the understanding that they were willing to lose money provided they got help from the stronger clubs," says Campbell. "There were some deals made in this regard, the haves trying to help the have-nots. But the only positive way to strengthen an organization at the time was through sponsored clubs, and here is where Tommy Ivan played a most important role in the revival of the Black Hawks."

Through the years, Montreal, Detroit and Toronto had produced great quantities of young talent by sponsoring amateur teams across Canada; for their investment, they acquired the professional rights to the youngsters playing on those teams. As a coach in Detroit, Ivan had watched players like Howe and Lindsay and Sawchuck rise out of the amateur leagues and, after a few years' seasoning, step with authority into Red Wing uniforms. As a result, when he moved to Chicago in 1954 at the urging of Jim Norris, Ivan knew the Hawks' future depended upon a farm system that didn't even exist:

"When I came over here," he recalls, "the Black Hawks had but one-half of a sponsored club. When sponsorships were abolished in 1970, we had nine. It took a lot of money, sweat and hustle to establish

Buffalo Sabres coach Joe Crozier watches tape of previous period on his closed-circuit television. Punch Imlach devised the system. It has proved invaluable.

that farm system. Jim said money was no object, but in the beginning not that many clubs were anxious to be sponsored by Chicago. We were tailenders at the time and people have their pride. Nobody wants to be associated with a loser. But I was always on the lookout for a club that might be interested, and when I heard of one, I was on a plane the next day.''

The Hawks continued to finish last through the 1957–58 season, but by then there was a ray of hope. Several, in fact. A young, blond left winger named Bobby Hull had made the club from the St. Catharines Juniors—a team Ivan had lined up after one of his plane trips. A goaltender named Glenn Hall had been acquired from Detroit. The next year two more prospects from St. Catharines, Stan Mikita and Ken Wharram, made the big team and the Hawks were on their way. They captured their second league championship in 1969–70 and the West Division title the three succeeding years. In 1971, they lost the Stanley Cup by one thin goal to Montreal in the seventh game of the play-off finals. Since 1957–58, Chicago has missed the play-offs only once and attendance has leaped

from 4,000 people to a raucous 22,000 per game.

"Sure, we did what we set out to do, but now the trick is staying here," says Ivan. "The only way you can do that is to make sure you're always bringing along good young talent. When sponsored clubs were abolished, we turned to the colleges. A lot of people were surprised when Keith Magnuson and Cliff Koroll made our club right out of Denver University. Frankly, we were a little surprised ourselves. But college players are here to stay and I'm seeing to it that we stay on top of them. I haven't missed an NCAA tournament in years.''

Another tough, driving member of the old school is George ("Punch") Imlach, who was coach and general manager of the Buffalo Sabres until a heart attack in January of 1972 forced him to give up coaching. Like Ivan, Imlach is crafty, cautious and drives a hard bargain. But he is also a colorful, flamboyant personality who wears fancy hats on his bald head and always has the needle out for the opposition. In Toronto, where he became the only man to win four Stanley Cups while combining the jobs of coach and general manager, Imlach operated in the classic tradition of the iron-fisted GM. He called the shots. *All* the shots. "I make the decisions myself," he said. "If the owners don't like it, they can fire me. I'll never forget what Conn Smythe told me when I took over his Leafs: 'Make your own mistakes.'" (Shortly after that, when Smythe offered to give Imlach some advice between periods of a game, Imlach snapped, "Look, I run the show. You watch it. As soon as you don't like it, just tell me to get the hell out.")

Eventually, Imlach was fired—but not until 11 years later, during which time his Leafs finished in first place once, second twice and made the play-offs 10 times. In 1962, 1963 and 1964, his teams won three Stanley Cups in a row and the owners and fans adored him. In 1965 and 1966, he missed winning it with the same players and there was talk of firing him. In 1967, they *really* wanted to fire Imlach when he stubbornly stuck by old players like Allan Stanley and George Armstrong and Tim Horton and Red Kelly. But after a 10-game winless streak at midseason left Toronto in fifth place and Imlach in the hospital with a case of severe exhaustion, the old Leafs fought their way back into the play-offs and went on to win their fourth Cup—the most satisfying one of all.

"He proved he was a real man during that ten-game streak," Horton said. "He could have blasted us in the papers and made a lot of lineup changes and taken us apart behind closed doors. But instead of criticizing us, he went out of his way to build up our confidence, and he kept impressing us with the fact that we had too much ability to keep skidding. In view of all the pressure that was on him to make changes, it took real patience and courage on his part to wait out the slump."

"I admit I may have carried sentiment to extremes with some of those players," Imlach says today. "But at the same time I don't think we'd have won that fourth Cup without those veterans. I've made moves, lots of moves, that I hated to make. But I always put the good of the hockey club first.

"I'll never forget the day, in 1964, I had to trade Dickie Duff. I called home with the news and my daughter answered the phone. When I told her what I'd done, she wouldn't speak to me for days. I'd had the audacity to trade away her favorite hockey player. Well, Dickie Duff was one of my favorites too, but I don't think we'd have won that year without Don McKenney, the man we got for Duff. I wanted that third Stanley Cup."

Frank Mahovlich wasn't one of Imlach's favorites, and the feeling was mutual. But on a cold October night in Toronto in 1962, it was Imlach who turned down a cool $1 million that Chicago owner Jim Norris was offering for Mahovlich. What transpired that night has since become one of the most celebrated "deals" in the history of all sport. Tommy Ivan was also there with Imlach, and both remember it well.

"It was the night before the annual All-Star Game," says Ivan. "We'd all been to dinner at the Royal York Hotel and had gone up to the governors' suite for a nightcap. There were a bunch of governors and executives around. I imagine every one of the six clubs was represented at one time or another. We were talking about a lot of things when Jim Norris and Harold Ballard, the executive vice-president of the Leafs, got on the subject of player value—just how much a player is worth to a club in terms of money. Jim said you can't place a dollar value on a player and Ballard said you can.

"They went on for a while and then Ballard asked Jim how much it would take to buy Bobby Hull, who had scored fifty goals and led the league in total points the year before. Jim said there was no way he would ever sell Bobby Hull—that you just can't attach a dollar value to a hockey player. Then Jim turned the discussion around. He asked Ballard if he would sell Frank Mahovlich, who had scored forty-eight and

thirty-three goals in his last two years. Frank and Bobby had been the All-Star left wingers the year before and were going to be the All-Star left wingers for a number of years to come. Ballard said he wouldn't sell Frank Mahovlich and Jim said, 'See, that's what I've been saying all along.'

"Then Ballard said, 'Well, everyone has his price.' They talked some more and finally Jim asked Ballard if he would take two hundred thousand dollars for Mahovlich. Ballard said no. The price went up to two hundred fifty thousand. Then four hundred and five hundred thousand. There was a lot of talk. Jim asked me what I thought of Mahovlich, if five hundred thousand was too much to offer for a hockey player like him. I said I didn't think it was. Then Jim offered seven hundred fifty thousand. I said I thought that was a little high, even though there was no doubt that Mahovlich was a helluva hockey player. Before long, they had worked the price up to a million dollars."

Imlach remembers the same evening.

"After the dinner, I was ready to go home and go to bed," he says. "But King Clancy, who was assistant general manager of the Leafs, and I had been invited up to a party that the governors were having in one of the hotel suites. We decided to go up for a few minutes. Well, as soon as I walked in the door Harold Ballard grabbed me and took me into another room. He closed the door behind him. Me, Clancy, Ballard and Jack Amell, a member of the Leafs' hockey committee, were there. 'Look,' Ballard said. 'Norris has offered us a million dollars for Mahovlich. What do you think?'

"I was a little shocked, but I hadn't been drinking at all. I told Ballard I wouldn't make the deal, that as a general manager I would make it but as a coach, no. 'A million dollars,' I said, 'can't play left wing for me.' "

"I remember that Ballard and Imlach went into the other room and closed the door," Ivan says. "While they were in there, Jim took out a piece of hotel stationery and wrote on it, 'I will pay the Toronto Maple Leafs one million dollars for Frank Mahovlich.' Then he signed his name. When Imlach and Ballard and the rest came out of the room, Norris gave Ballard the paper and said, 'Sign this.' Ballard and Amell wrote 'accepted' on the piece of paper and signed their names.

"Then Jim said, 'How much earnest money do you want?' Ballard said they didn't need any, that Jim's word was good enough for them. But Jim still reached in his pocket, pulled out his roll and peeled off, gosh, I think it was thirty one-hundred-dollar bills. He gave the money to Ballard.''

"Ballard wanted me to shake hands with Norris to seal the deal," says Imlach. "Neither he nor Amell, you see, had the power to make the deal. Nobody did except me, the general manager. Of course, they could have fired me and then made the deal if they had wanted to. But I was adamant. I wouldn't shake hands on the deal. I told them I wasn't going to do anything more about it that night. I have a policy; I like to talk about deals over a drink or two, but I wait until the next day before I do anything concrete.

"But Ballard wouldn't take no for an answer. The discussion got pretty heated and there was some argument, but I don't think Norris was upset at me for tossing a roadblock into things. He knew I was the general manager of the Maple Leafs and that I was only trying to do my job. But by now, word had gotten around the room that Norris and Ballard had signed a piece of paper concluding the sale of Frank Mahovlich to Chicago for a million dollars. There was a lot of loud talk and discussion. Finally I just left. There was nothing more I was going to do that night.''

"By now it was about twelve-thirty in the morning," says Ivan. "Jim had signed the paper and given Ballard the earnest money. So he said, 'Well, how do we release it?' Ballard said that there were Toronto newspapermen in the other room. They agreed to release it within the hour. Jim had me get on the phone back to our publicity man in Chicago with the announcement that the Black Hawks had just purchased left winger Frank Mahovlich of the Toronto Maple Leafs for one million dollars. It made the *Tribune* the next morning.''

"I heard it over the car radio on my way home," says Imlach. "They interrupted a program with the news. Of course, you've got to understand what a deal like that meant. Nothing like it before had ever happened in hockey. I later found out that phones were ringing all over that suite where the governors were, that everybody and his mother was being interviewed and was giving his feelings on the deal. There's just never been anything like it before. And even though the World Series was going on between the Yankees and the Giants in San Francisco, the Mahovlich deal was the big story across Canada and especially in Toronto and Chicago.''

"The next morning," Ivan recalls, "I went down to Jim's suite pretty early and asked him if he still wanted to close the deal we'd made the night before. He said sure, by all means. We went down and had some orange juice and coffee. Jim pulled out his checkbook and said he'd just write out a check so I could take it over to Maple Leaf Gardens. I said no, I'd get it typed up. So he gave me a blank check and I took it down to the assistant manager's office in the Royal York and asked if I might have the services of his secretary for a few minutes. He said his secretary was off, it was a Saturday, but he got me a fellow who could type. I told the guy I didn't want any mistakes, that I had something pretty important. When I told him I wanted a check typed out for one million dollars, you should have seen the look on his face. For a minute, I know he thought I was crazy.

"When the check was finally typed up, I went back upstairs to Jim's suite and he signed it. I walked downstairs, got in a cab and went over to Maple Leaf Gardens. It was about nine-thirty in the morning when I walked into Stafford Smythe's office. He was there with King Clancy and Amell. I walked over and tossed the check on Staff's desk. 'Here's the check for the deal we made last night,' I said. He picked it up, looked at it and tossed it back in front of me. 'We can't make this kind of a deal until we've had a meeting of the board of directors.' I told him that we'd made a deal and a deal's a deal. He insisted he couldn't make it.

"I asked him if I could use his phone and he said sure. I called Jim on the phone and, well, let's just say that he was upset, He said, *'We made a deal!'* So I put him on the phone with Staff and their discussion got pretty hot. We never got Mahovlich, but that's how the whole thing happened.''

"I'd talked to Stafford," says Imlach, "and told him that there was no deal. I'd thought the whole thing through and, as I said, a million bucks does a coach no good on left wing. Or on the power play. But it was two weeks before the thing finally died down. The publicity surrounding it was fantastic. The NHL has often been accused of an October publicity stunt in an effort to grab some of that newspaper space that always goes to the World Series. I won't deny that it happens, but this time it was no stunt. The Mahovlich deal was real. It was just that I, as general manager, wouldn't make it.

"But who could blame Jim Norris? What was a million dollars to him? His club had already won one Stanley Cup, and if he had Mahovlich to go with Hull and Mikita and the rest of those gunners, who could

Tough bargainer Tommy Ivan, general manager of Chicago, helped build the present team. It includes defenseman Pat Stapleton, left, and All-Star Bill White, 2.

stop them? Certainly not Toronto. As it turned out, Toronto went on to win three straight Cups. I admit I often looked back on that deal and wondered—especially in the 1962–63 season—where we and Chicago would have finished if they'd gotten Mahovlich. We finished in first place and they wound up second—one point behind us.

"I've never been offered that type of an arrangement in which the owner makes the decisions and the GM takes the heat. But if I was, I'd have to say that for one-hundred-fifty thousand dollars a year I'll be your fall guy. For seventy-five thousand dollars I'll be your general manager."

In the next few years, it was Imlach's Maple Leafs, Montreal and Chicago that sparred for the NHL championship and the Stanley Cup. Then, in October of 1964, a pale, gaunt former goaltender was appointed general manager of the New York Rangers, a team whose lackluster history was soon to undergo an abrupt turn for the better. The career of Emile Percy ("Cat") Francis had been rich only in mediocrity. In 14 years he had played for 12 clubs and only briefly in the NHL. But after spending several years managing outlaw baseball teams in his hometown of North Battleford, Saskatchewan, he began prepping for Broadway with the Rangers' farm club in Guelph, Ontario. Francis took command in New York in 1964 with enthusiasm, a sharp hockey mind and an open checkbook from owner Bill Jennings.

Though no bigger than a parking meter, Francis thought big. After watching his diminutive Rangers get slammed around the old Madison Square Garden for a few games, Francis made a few long-distance phone calls and roughnecks like Reg Fleming, Orland Kurtenbach and Wayne Hillman were putting on the Broadway blue. Smaller players were immediately weeded from the farm system. "After a season is over, you usually send the uniforms your NHL club has worn down to the minor-league club, so they can wear them the following year," says Francis. "Well there'd been such a trend to bigger players in our farm system that first year that when they tried on those uniforms the next season, they didn't fit."

Then Francis started dealing for the future. He shipped Andy Bathgate, New York's all-time scoring leader and only legitimate star, to Toronto in exchange for Rod Seiling, Arnie Brown and Bob Nevin—all of whom would play major roles in lifting the Rangers into the ranks of the contenders. In Providence, Rhode Island, Francis found a goalie named Ed

Giacomin, and in the years to come his rebuilt farm system would start producing players like Walt Tkaczuk, Brad Park and Bill Fairbairn.

When Red Sullivan was fired as coach in 1965, Francis took over. The standard joke was that the Cat had crawled out onto a hot tin roof. But at the end of the following season, the Rangers were in the play-offs for the first time in five years and future stars like Jean Ratelle and Rod Gilbert were beginning to shine.

Up at 6 A.M., rarely home on Long Island before midnight, Francis worked like a draft horse. If there was no game at night, there was practice in the morning—and Francis had a team trainer pick him up and chauffeur him to the rink so that he could handle paper work on the way. After practice he was then driven downtown to his office in Madison Square Garden. On the road Francis logged more than 75,000 miles a year, running the Rangers from behind the bench, scouting and keeping an eye on his minor-league operation. "If New York's in here on a Thursday night," said Scotty Bowman, then coach of the St. Louis Blues, "you can bet Emile will be in Omaha on Wednesday night, watching his farm club."

But just how could he kick the Rangers into contention so quickly? "The first thing we had to do was knock all the excuses out of the hat," Francis recalls. "There were so many excuses for losing in New York. The city, the commute, the anonymity. *Anonymity!* Hell, who wants to be recognized if he's a loser? I sure as hell don't. If I'm a loser, I don't want anybody to know who I am. We told them to start winning and they'd be recognized soon enough."

When Imlach was forced to give up coaching Buffalo following his heart attack, Francis was the only man left in the NHL wearing the hats of both coach and general manager. But in spite of the general feeling that handling both jobs is too much for one individual, Francis argues, "I like it just the way it is. In my position I'm able to influence what's going on with the club in its two most critical areas—on the ice and in the future. As a coach, you tend to do things that will get you immediate results. But as general manager, you've got to be concerned with the future. So when I'm combining both jobs, I'm actually doing what's best for the club from two directions.''

On several occasions, the Rangers have flirted with what would be their first division title since 1942; the closest they came was in 1967–68, when they finished only four points behind Montreal. A number of times they have roared into January at the top of the standings, only to eventually slide back into the standings. Their play-off record has been one of frustration. New York has reached the finals only once under Francis, in 1972, when the Rangers were eliminated by Boston in six games. "We've come close but still no cigar," Francis says wistfully. "But I can remember when the Rangers weren't even close. We can't quit now."

Of course, for years the Rangers' constant companions at the bottom of the standings were the Boston Bruins. In fact, in two decades following the departure of Art Ross, the Bruins managed to make the play-off finals only four times. It was not a crafty, energetic general manager who lifted the Bruins from the basement; most of the credit for that goes to a young, dishwater blond from Parry Sound, Ontario, named Bobby Orr. However, there are three other players who weren't exactly along for the ride—Phil Esposito, Ken Hodge and Fred Stanfield—and they were acquired from the Chicago Black Hawks in 1967 by Milt Schmidt, then Boston's general manager. With the exception of Orr, the addition of these three players did more to revive the Bruins than anything else did.

What prompted the trade was the disenchantment of both Tommy Ivan and coach Billy Reay with Esposito, who had failed to score a point in the 1967 play-off semifinals against Toronto. Chicago had run away with the NHL title that year and had high hopes of topping it off with a Stanley Cup. But instead, they were eliminated in six games by the Maple Leafs.

Meanwhile, Schmidt, in his first year as GM of the Bruins, a team that had missed the play-offs for the eighth season in a row, was in the market for bigger forwards. After weeks of consultation, the two clubs finally announced the deal on May 15—just five minutes before the trading deadline. The Black Hawks sent Esposito, Hodge and Stanfield to Boston for center Pit Martin, defenseman Gilles Marotte and goalie Jack Norris. Within a year the Bruins were in the play-offs, and by 1970 they had their first Stanley Cup since 1941. Just the reverse was to happen in Chicago—two years after the trade the Black Hawks were in last place.

Even though the Hawks have since come back to win one East and three West Division titles in four years, Tommy Ivan has never been able to live down the Esposito trade. "Really, I have chosen not to comment on it at all," he says. "Almost anything I would say could be interpreted as an alibi or as sour grapes. I don't believe in living in the past. That can be disastrous, because every minute you're living in the past is a minute you should be spending on the present or the future. You learn from the past; when you make a bad deal, and I've made some bad deals, you just roll up your sleeves and try to do better. If you fail again, at least you can say you tried."

And because Ivan tried again, one of the most one-sided trades in hockey history was hardly a disaster for the Black Hawks. Martin has proved himself to be a steady scorer and playmaker as a five-year regular, and by eventually dealing the disappointing Marotte to Los Angeles, Ivan acquired an excellent defenseman in Bill White. He also got goalie Gerry Desjardins, who was later picked by the New York Islanders (for $250,000) in the 1972 expansion draft.

"It's funny," says Schmidt, a tall, classy former NHL All-Star, now 55 years old. "As a player I thought I knew it all. As a coach I found out I didn't. As a general manager, I found out I didn't know as much as I thought when I was a coach. And I'm not about to tell you now that I know the bylaws, the ins and outs of being a general manager, the way Sam Pollock does.

"But when we made that deal with Chicago, we needed beef up front. That's what we wanted in the deal and that's what we got. There was no reason to believe that Esposito was going to score seventy-six goals. Gilles Marotte was the man they wanted, and people tend to forget that when the deal was made, Marotte was a pretty hot item. He'd just had a good year for us and we weren't at all anxious to get rid of him. Tommy's had a rough go from the writers and fans about that trade. What they fail to realize is that it could happen to anyone."

Schmidt was in fact wondering what was happening to him in 1972 when, just before the season started, he had suddenly been graced with the title of "executive director" with the return of Harry Sinden, who would be "managing director." Sinden, of course, was the man who had coached Boston to its first Stanley Cup in 29 years in 1970, only to quit three days later when the Bruins failed to boost him from $22,000 to $30,000. After spending two years as an executive with a New York housing firm, which eventually went bankrupt, Sinden returned to Boston, apparently to share the general manager's duties with Schmidt. Initially shocked at the disclosure of the front office changes, Schmidt thought it over and said, "I'm really happy with the changes. I'm anxious to work with Harry. All I want to do now is get my duties clarified."

No general manager in recent years has gone through what Ned Harkness went through in Detroit in 1970–71. The Red Wings' front office upheaval was so vicious, confusing and emotional that even Gordie Howe was upset.

Actually it had all started back in 1962, when owner Bruce Norris decided that Jack Adams should retire after more than 30 years as GM. He replaced him with Sid Abel. (Though well-cared-for financially, Adams never forgave the Wings and died still feeling bitter a few years later.) A former All-Star center and member of the famed "Production Line" with Howe and Lindsay, Abel inherited a powerful organization from Adams. Abel was a good coach, but unlike the Imlachs and the Francises, he found combining it with the general managership not to his liking. Abel enjoys his free time and makes sure he gets it; he even invested in some race horses, an interest shared by Bruce Norris.

Although the Red Wings did not dominate the NHL in the early sixties, they were respectable. They made the play-offs with consistency, and in 1964–65 they shocked the league with another title when Abel talked Ted Lindsay out of retirement for a last hurrah. But at the same time, the bluebloods of the fifties were aging fast. To make up for it Abel started exchanging youth from the Detroit farm system for established players. In 1966–67, everything caught up with him all at once when Detroit missed the play-offs for the first time in four straight seasons. In 1967–68, the Wings finished at the bottom of the East Division and surrendered a whopping 257 goals—more than any other club in the league. Bill Gadsby, a former Ranger and Red Wing, took over as coach in 1968–69. The Wings finished badly again, but there were signs of improvement. And then, after Detroit opened the next season with two straight victories, Norris mysteriously fired Gadsby, saying that the Wings needed a "more sophisticated" coach. While the search for one got underway, Abel went behind the bench again and the Wings wound up in third place—only to be eliminated from the play-offs in four games by Chicago.

Enter Ned Harkness, an outrageously successful college hockey coach at Rensselaer Polytechnic Institute and Cornell University. Norris, in concert with Jim Bishop, whom he had recently hired as the club's "executive director," felt that Harkness was just what the Wings needed, a perfect blend of strength, savvy —and sophistication.

Harkness comes on strong and always has. Even in the egg business in Troy, New York, he admits, he was a pusher. "I was aggressive, a positive thinker, a hustler," Harkness recalls. "I had to be. When you're dealing in terms of a quarter-cent on the dozen, you've got to be aggressive if you hope to survive."

First at RPI, then at Cornell, Harkness forged winning teams with methods that greatly unnerved his rivals. He would do anything to win. Once, when his outmanned RPI players were losing to a superior opponent, the normal 10 minutes between periods strangely drifted into 30 with the playing of both schools' alma maters and trophy presentations to various RPI athletes, all of whom were encouraged to say a few words. Another time RPI was losing in the third period of a game when suddenly all the lights went out. Over an electric public address system that worked perfectly, the crowd was informed that there had been a power failure in the building. Then there was the RPI rink itself, where the ice always seemed on the slushy side when a fast-skating opponent came in. Harkness, of course, denies there were any shenanigans.

"Sure he's a double-talker," recalled one of Harkness's Cornell players. "He'd come up to me before a game and say, 'Harry, we can't win this one without you,' and I'd get all fired up. Then he'd stop and say the same thing to another guy who was just out of earshot."

Then there was Harkness the recruiter, who was despised for going across the border into Canada for his hockey players. "He'd snow you with stories about Cornell," says another player, "and then he'd get to your parents and it would be all over. Before you knew it, *they* were trying to talk you into going to school at Cornell."

So the year after his Cornell team won the national championship, going undefeated in 29 straight games, Harkness was the new coach of the Detroit Red Wings. With sophistication, he informed the Delvecchios and the Stemkowskis and the Bergmans that smoking in public was taboo. Garry Unger was told that long locks were to be shorn. Curfews would be respected and enforced with bed checks. It was not a case of love at first sight, especially after the easy ship Abel had commanded. "Am I hearing this right?" one Red Wing veteran muttered. "All of this, from *him*? A guy who never played a shift in the National Hockey League?"

Predictably, Abel and Harkness clashed immediately and the team sank to the bottom of the standings, where it would remain for the duration of the season. By early January, Abel was in Norris's office, asking whether he had the authority to fire Harkness. Upon being informed that he did not, Abel thought it over for a few hours and resigned. Later that same night, Gordie Howe went to Norris and, speaking for himself and the players, said that the team could no longer play for Harkness. The next day Harkness was elevated to general manager, replacing Abel, and Doug Barkley was rushed in from the Red Wings' Fort Worth farm team to coach. Then the housecleaning began. Pete Stemkowski, Bruce MacGregor and Dale Rolfe went to New York. Frank Mahovlich departed for Montreal. Garry Unger and Wayne Connelly were shipped to St. Louis. In return, however, Harkness was getting players such as Red Berenson, Tim Ecclestone, Guy Charron, Mickey Redmond and

Bill Collins. As it turned out, finishing in last place was a blessing in disguise—the Red Wings were able to pick Marcel Dionne in the amateur draft, a youngster who would score 28 goals and set an NHL record for points (77) by a rookie. When Barkley quit during the 1971–72 season, Harkness tapped Johnny Wilson, a former Red Wing who had coached at Princeton University. Under Wilson, the Wings marshaled a drive that fell just short of a play-off spot, and the following year—with Dionne leading the way—they were a contender once again.

What was it like for Harkness, a gung-ho college man, moving into the furtive company of the Ivans, the Pollocks and the Imlachs? "I won't deny that I was regarded with suspicion and, in some cases, with scorn," he says. "After all, I was the new kid on the block. But the first thing I did was to sit down, call every one of them up and say, 'Look, we're in trouble. I'm willing to deal anybody but Howe and Delvecchio. Got any suggestions?' I've never run across anyone, be he an egg buyer or an NHL general manager, who wasn't willing to deal if he thought the price was right."

Meanwhile, Abel filtered down to St. Louis, where the departure of Scotty Bowman in May of 1971 had just left the Blues in the hands of the owners, young Sid Salomon III and his father, Sid, Jr. Like Jack Kent Cooke in Los Angeles and Charles O. Finley in Oakland, the Salomons prefer to run their team as they see fit. General managers who work for such owners do so in title only.

In Minnesota, however, Wren Blair speaks for himself. And he's earned the right; he literally talked his way out of a Beaton's Dairy milk truck in Oshawa and into the GM's chair of the Minnesota North Stars. In 1952, Blair showed up at a meeting of the Ontario Hockey Association and introduced himself as head of a group that wanted senior hockey for Oshawa. He was awarded a team.

"But it's one thing to have a team and another thing to finance it," he recalls. "All the players were being paid back then and I spent the entire summer signing them up—even though I had no sponsor and no money to meet salaries or buy equipment. Things were getting pretty desperate, almost to the point where I was going to have to give my players their contracts back. Finally, I took a Friday afternoon off from work and tried one last time to find a sponsor."

Turned down everywhere, Blair was on the south side of town about 5 P.M. when he noticed the head office of Smith Transport along the highway. "I pulled

Above: Punch Imlach keeps busy in his role as general manager. A heart attack forced him out of his first love, coaching. *Opposite:* Rangers' GM Emile Francis dealt for size and muscle when he acquired Ted Irvine, 27.

hundred-fifty thousand dollars—a tidy little profit."

Obviously, there is no formula for attaining success, or even security, as a general manager. The difference could be as close as the telephone or as far in the future as a three-year-old trying out his first pair of skates.

Says Sam Pollock, "You work around the clock to get what you have, then you work around the clock to keep it. When you're down, maybe you're inclined to gamble. When you're on top, you're inclined to be selfish. It kills me to see my hockey club lose, and I know every other manager in the league feels the same way. And whenever you're responsible for the overall operation of something as large as a professional hockey club, it's inevitable that you're going to have to do some things that you hate to do. One of the hardest things I've had to do in all my years with the Canadiens was replace Claude Ruel as coach in 1970. Claude is a very close personal friend.

"But Claude is now our director of player development—one of the biggest jobs in the entire organization. I've always felt that there are at least two or three jobs a person can do for an organization; I've held a lot of jobs with the Canadiens myself. But you don't go around hiring and firing and shifting people around just to shake things up. Here in Montreal, we've been extremely fortunate in getting people who were loyal and friendly toward each other and who were willing to do almost anything that was asked of them."

"When you become a general manager, you know you'll never get the job done," says Tommy Ivan. "I mean, after you win the division title and the Cup one year, you've got the next year to worry about. Me, I just try to keep myself from getting too high over a victory and too low over a defeat. I try to remain on an even keel emotionally. It's self-preservation, really, because your emotions can kill you in this business.

"I try to cover all bets. I want to know everything about everybody in this game, because you never know when it might help you make a sounder decision. I have two lines into my telephone at home; if somebody calls me, I want to know what he wants to talk about. Once I know what it is, maybe we'll talk the next day, but at least I know why he called in the first place.

"This is a strange business. I've seen a lot of strange things happen. You never can tell when someone just might want to give you another Bobby Orr."

over with, we started drafting from their unprotected lists and dropping Reg Fleming from our roster. We figured that, considering the needs of the other clubs, Fleming was the least likely player we'd lose. We got Ron Zaine, Tom Miller and Ken Murray this way. We had René Robert too, but when we then moved him from our protected list, Pittsburgh grabbed him and I wound up having to trade them Eddie Shack to get him back.

"Anyway, Zaine made our Buffalo club that year while Miller and Murray went down and helped our Cincinnati farm club make the play-offs. In all, it cost us one-hundred-twenty thousand dollars for those players, but when they all were picked in the expansion draft the following year, we got about seven-

After one year at the Rangers' helm, Emile Francis guided his team into the play-offs. Jean Ratelle (19), with teammates Vic Hadfield and Rod Gilbert *(above)*, became the dominant offensive force in New York.

5 | A Private Hell

What is worst for a goaltender: a Bobby Hull slap shot, an Esposito deflection, the five-against-three power play or the injuries? Surprisingly, none of them. Four goalies—Ken Dryden, Gump Worsley, Cesare Maniago and Jacques Plante—talk about the pain, the fear, the anxiety, the torment—why theirs is the hardest job in all sport.

The hardest part is the waiting. The frozen rubber leaping from the sticks of Hull, Lemaire, Orr, is bad. But not as bad as the waiting. Awakening from a fitful sleep, tasteless toast and eggs, the Sheraton lobby, team meetings. Then a steak and back to the room for the remaining hours; a nap, perhaps, but more likely the drone and flicker of television—"The Dating Game," "General Hospital," "The Secret Storm." Game day. Waiting. The private hell of the goaltenders.

"I've been fortunate all the years," says Jacques Plante. "After I have my steak I go to bed, and I sleep for those hours, so during that time I don't think about the game. When I get up, I get dressed and go to the rink. I don't have that much time to think. If I couldn't sleep on the day of a game maybe I would not have lasted so long as a goaltender."

Goaltenders' tales of anguish go back to the very beginning of professional hockey. All the shots. Some you see, some you don't. Some you don't see you stop, some you do see and don't stop. Slap shots, screen shots, deflections. Reflection and dejection. Big games, meaningless games. Hot last night, cold tonight, maybe finished tomorrow. Injuries.

The position of goaltender in hockey is the most difficult position in all of sport. It shows. One night, after the red light had gone on too many times behind him, goaltender Frank Brimsek of Boston was walking home with a teammate when a fire engine roared by, its red light flashing in the darkness. "Oh no," Brimsek shuddered. "Oh no . . . get me outa here!"

Another night Wilfie Cude of Detroit was enjoying a quiet steak dinner with his wife when she happened to ask how a particular goal had been scored on him. Cude slowly rose from the table, picked up the steak and, without a word, hurled it against a wall.

Montreal's Bill Durnan was one of the best goaltenders in the history of the game. He won the cherished Vezina Trophy six times. He was in the nets for numerous championships and Stanley Cups. But in the midst of the 1950 play-offs, Durnan asked his coach, Dick Irvin, to replace him. He never played again. "It had gotten so bad that I couldn't sleep the night before a game," Durnan explained. "I couldn't keep my meals down. The job—it was with me all the time, wherever I went. Nothing is worth that kind of agony."

The stories abound. Hockey fans read them and

Most goaltenders agree that theirs is the world's worst job. *Preceding pages:* Ken Dryden gets beaten. *Right:* Kings' Gary Edwards makes the stop.

IAVILLI

Clockwise from left above: Gilles Villemure takes needed refreshment; Ed Giacomin sprawls after making the save as Sanderson darts after rebound; Gerry Desjardins makes the catch amid chaos; Tony Esposito watches the puck sail over his head.

know them. All goalies know the torture. It gave Bruce Gamble of Philadelphia a heart attack in the second period of a game against Vancouver. He finished out the game.

Glenn Hall, an All-Star goaltender with Detroit, Chicago and St. Louis, isn't sure if he'll write a book about his career. But he has the title—*There'll Be No Slap Shots in Heaven.* Over the years Hall became as famous for the food he couldn't keep down as for the pucks he kept out. "They say that no one can say a word to the man before a game," former teammate Lou Angotti once needled Hall in a restaurant. "Even a sneeze and he has to use the bucket. But I'd talk to him. I'd walk right up to him and tell him, 'You'd better be sick, Hall. You'd better be sick 'cause they're going to take *sixty* shots at you tonight.' "

Hall smiled thinly and said, "With you out there Louie, they usually do."

Kenneth Wayne Dryden is a tall, scholarly graduate of Cornell University. He attends law school at McGill University in Montreal, and during the summer of 1971, he worked for "Nader's Raiders" in Washington, D.C. Ken Dryden is also the goaltender for the Montreal Canadiens. Since he anchored the Canadiens in their stunning upset of the Boston Bruins in the 1971 Stanley Cup play-offs (for which he was voted the series' most valuable player), Dryden has become the finest young goaltender in the National Hockey League. He was one of the goaltenders for Team Canada in its memorable eight-game series against the Soviet Union in the fall of 1972. Having lost two games and won a third against the Russians, Dryden had the unnerving task of tending goal for the eighth and final game—with the series knotted at three wins apiece and one tie.

"When you think about a goaltender's job, just think about myself and [Russia's] Vladislav Tretiak going into that eighth game in Moscow," says Dryden. "I mean, both of us had the worst job in the world going into that game. I think back and remember that we'd won the seventh game with Tony [Esposito] to tie the series, and all of a sudden, five minutes after winning that game, all the excitement was over for me. I was playing the *eighth* game. In two days I was going to be playing the eighth and deciding game in . . . well, it was quite apparent what the series meant to Canada and Russia.

"I'd get it from guys on the club. They felt the pressure, and they knew what I was feeling. They'd come up and say things. Like Phil Esposito said,

'Well, I don't want to put the pressure on you but you'd better be hot.' And for two days I've never had such an uncertain feeling. It never left. Even when my thoughts couldn't be further away from hockey— just walking down the street—my legs just weren't functioning right. It was horrible. I literally had the worst job in the bloody world going into that game.

"Fortunately, this kind of thing doesn't happen that often. I can see why those bloody guys quit early. The only time I've felt something similar was that seventh game in Boston in 1971. The night before I was very uneasy. That was the night I watched the Bruins' highlights on television. In a highlights' film you mostly see goals. And it looks like you can't stop a thing. You're sort of looking back and thinking, 'Gee, I thought I looked better on that.' You realize that they're highlights, but at the same time you don't like to see goals scored on you."

Lorne ("Gump") Worsley is a short, squat, crew-cut fellow of 43, who looks like he should be tending bar instead of goal. He became a legend in New York, facing 50 shots a game for the hapless Rangers. In Montreal, he seemed to reach his peak in the pres-

"There are moments out there when you just feel great." *Above:* Jacques Caron beats the Rangers. *Left:* Ken Dryden makes spectacular save. *Opposite:* Gary Edwards relaxes.

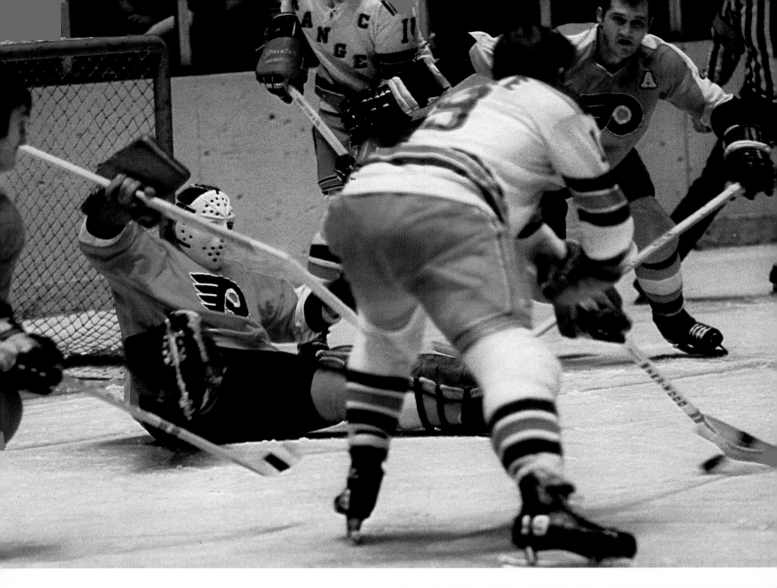

Clockwise from above: Doug Favell thwarts Rangers rush; Rene Robert pulls the string on Flames' goalie Phil Myre; Tony Esposito in isolated dejection as his team loses the Stanley Cup semifinals; Gump Worsley makes stop.

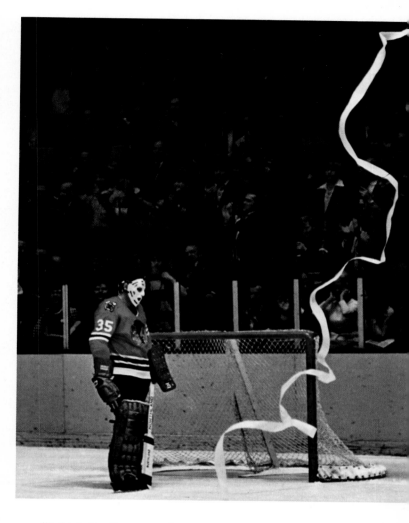

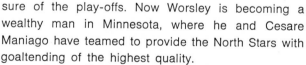

sure of the play-offs. Now Worsley is becoming a wealthy man in Minnesota, where he and Cesare Maniago have teamed to provide the North Stars with goaltending of the highest quality.

Normally, the Gumper is cheerful, quick, curious and witty. He likes people and enjoys their company in a restaurant, a nightclub, a hotel lobby or a coffee shop. But on game day, forget it.

"The waiting is murder," said Worsley one game day. He was sitting in the lobby of the Chase-Park Plaza in St. Louis, working on a crossword puzzle with teammate Murray Oliver. His face was pale and unshaven, and his mood was not cheerful.

"During the game you can't worry about what's going to happen because you're worrying about what's happening right then," he said. "But sitting around, waiting for a big game, especially a play-off game, is murder. All you do is worry what's going to happen, but there's nothing you can do about it—not then.

"I think it all comes down to a guy's temperament. Some are high-strung and others, like me, are not. I'm not as uptight on game days as some goaltenders. A guy like Glenn [Hall] threw up before a game, but he did it all the time, so they let him do it and didn't worry about it. That's Glenn. Me, if I throw up before a game, they ask me if I'm sick. People are different, everyone knows that. But let's face it, we goaltenders are a breed apart."

Cesare Maniago is a tall, polite, brown-eyed man of 34, who also used to play for the Rangers, but who came into his own only after the North Stars picked him in the 1967 expansion draft. Maniago was a workhorse, playing as many as 64 games in one year, but his goals-against average improved to a solid 2.66 after Worsley was obtained in 1971. Maniago and Worsley are close friends.

"Gump and I have been rooming together ever since he came to the club," Maniago says. "And it's

proven good for us. We understand each other. I know what's going through his mind; he knows what's going through mine. Take today, for instance. Gump is playing tonight, so I know it's no use talking to him. If I'm going to discuss anything, it'll be anything but hockey. I know that I try to relax as much as I can the day of a game, but relaxation just isn't there. I'm concentrating on hockey too much, building myself up to the game.

"Gump and I have the same thoughts on the day of a game. We'll discuss the weather, baseball, football or golf. But not hockey. The goalie for that night goes through the game in his own mind so it's no use going into it any further. If I concentrate too much on the game, I get sick to my stomach."

Jacques Plante has been a goaltender longer than anyone in the National Hockey League—since 1953. By everyone's standards, he is one of the best who ever lived; many say he is *the* best. Now 44, Jacques Plante has played for Montreal, New York, St. Louis and now Toronto, and he has pioneered in the art of keeping the puck out of the net. He was the first to roam from the goal crease to clear the puck or to stop it behind the net for a teammate. He was the first goaltender to wear a mask. Often accused of being a showboat on the ice, which he is, Plante is a loner off it—an intelligent, reflective man of quiet Gallic dignity. The cheeks are sunken, the hair liberally flecked with gray, but many of the scars from playing the years before the mask are almost gone.

"The first big game I ever played was in the play-offs in 1953, when I was new with Montreal," Plante remembers. "We were playing Chicago, and we were behind 3–2 in games. We were in Chicago, and if we lost that game we were out of the play-offs. Dick Irvin told me just before the game, after I had gotten up from my sleep, 'Jacques, you're playing tonight and you better get a shutout.'

"I went to the rink in a daze. Putting on my equipment, I started to shake. I tried to lace up my skates, and I couldn't do it, I was shivering so much. I didn't think I could play that game.

"I still get that feeling. I'm playing tonight, and I'm not really relaxed. It may look like I am, because I'm not thinking about it. It's when I'm alone. I know who I'm going to face tonight and who gives me the most trouble. But the time I feel it most is just prior to the game, when I'm sitting and waiting. I get butterflies, and shivers go between my shoulder blades. I

"There is no way I would ever play without a mask," Dryden insists. "Absolutely no way." Andy Brown *(opposite and above)* is one of two NHL goalies who do.

145

"I'm not afraid to get hurt. I expect it." At moments like this—Ted Irvine crashing into Dunc Wilson—goaltenders can incur serious harm.

"I could have gone out at them, but it would have been wrong." Ken Dryden holds his ground against Lou Angotti, forces the Chicago center in too close, makes the save and trips up Angotti.

start to sweat. It's a cold sweat. It's a feeling I can hardly describe."

"On the morning of a game you more or less go over the guys you're facing that night," says Maniago. "Naturally, you think of the ones with the harder or tougher shots, the ones that are a little more dangerous in front of the net, the defensemen that like to shoot a lot from the point, those that would rather pass off, and so forth. We normally have a noon meeting the day of the game, but by then I've already been preparing myself. Jack [Gordon] normally tells us the day before a game whether Gump or I am going to start. That gives us an opportunity to prepare for the game in our own way."

"One of the most interesting things about the last two years is that so many of the preconceptions that I had about preparing for a game, I've really thrown out the window," says Dryden. "I mean, you go to sleep the night before a game at a certain time, you get up at a certain time, you eat a certain meal, you take a nap in the afternoon before the game, then you play. The fascinating thing is that so many times this kind of schedule has been disrupted. The first time it happens, you think, 'Oh my gosh, I didn't sleep as long as I was supposed to. I won't have time to do this or make up for that.' But I've found that you go out there, and it makes absolutely no difference in the world.

"Another thing: If you're injured or slightly injured, you're still playing. This can be most disruptive, because it detracts from a goalie's total concentration. If he has a slightly pulled muscle, he will worry about pulling it more, maybe not being able to move as well, this sort of thing."

"You've got to concentrate on the game itself," says Maniago. "You can't worry about the puck and how hard it's coming. If your knee's going to give out when you split; if, when you move your leg one way, you are going to leave yourself open—you just can't worry. You'll do something to keep yourself from worrying—wearing the mask to protect your face, putting a piece of fiber at the knee joint to help you split."

"There are times when the pressure gets unbearable," says Dryden. "There are times during certain games, big games, when you've really got to be sharp. Oftentimes it depends on the team. I know last year the Canadiens seemed to start off a game slowly. It was my prime job to keep our team ahead, even or no more than one goal behind at the end of the first period. If I did that, we'd win most of our games. Tony Esposito of Chicago said that one of the best things he does is to read his own club. He knows when they're going to be ready and when they're not, so he knows when he's going to have to be especially good. I think I'm the same way. I can tell before a game if we're ready. If not, I'm not surprised by a couple of goals. I know that a team like Montreal is good enough to come out of it and get those goals back.

"You go into each game with a bit of uncertainty. But, to a degree, I think you just wipe that all out as you gain an overall confidence, knowing just how well you're going to react. In the warm-up you can tell a bit, but not totally. So much depends just how things happen in a game. You can be really hot in a warm-up, get two impossible chances early in the game and be behind 2–0 before you know what happened. Then you're sort of down when there's no reason to be down. Hopefully, early in the game, you won't have the impossible chance. You'll have the difficult chance and make the save, and all of a sudden you have the feeling of well-being. It's totally psychological, because you can do it physically almost all the time. But when you get that feeling of well-being, you're pretty tough to beat."

To Worsley, embarrassment is the key. Whether the game is played before a national television audience or a home-town crowd of 15,000 people, no hockey player likes to look bad. And no player is as vulnerable as the goalie. "You're the last line of defense," Worsley explains. "That's why there's more pressure on you than anybody else. When the goaltender makes a mistake, they mark it up on the scoreboard. Oh, they can say tough shot, he was screened, things like that. But you're still the one the puck got by."

Maniago agrees with his teammate. While he waits, he worries about possible embarrassment. When the team has an off-night, only the goaltender can prevent a big score. "You don't worry about getting hurt," he adds. "You worry that they don't get too many goals against you."

"The more you play, the more you understand why guys like Bill Durnan acted the way they did," muses Dryden. "You really are a focal point out there. You're the only guy playing that position, except for the man two-hundred feet away. You're conspicuous. When things are going well, you get more than your share of credit, but when they're not, you

also get a lot more than your share of the abuse."

Jacques Plante fears a bad game. Like most goaltenders, he can brush aside a well-earned goal. But, as he explains, "Even though I have played a long time in the nets, if a bad goal is scored on me, I will think about it. I will think about it even though I try to erase it. Goaltenders don't fear injury as much as they fear playing a bad game. We're all afraid of playing a bad game, because if we have a bad game we're going to lose."

"When they stick four or five behind you, it depends on how the team plays and how you play," says Dryden. "Sure you're frustrated, but the cause of the letdown is what you think about. Four or five goals you don't shrug off. Four, five goals a team like Montreal shouldn't give up. If it's more team fault than personal fault, then you're thinking, 'Why did we play that way? There's no reason for us to play that way. We're better than that.' Now if it's personal fault, then it's 'Jeez Murphy, I just wasn't concentrating at that time. My mind was wandering. I can't do that.'

"You agonize. With the Russians, I was really wondering, 'Have these guys got my number?' I played against them once, prior to the Team Canada series, and they bombed me. Then they beat me twice again. I wasn't ready to believe it was totally my fault, but it's easier to rationalize one time than three."

"You have pressure no matter what team you play for," says Plante. "When you play for a winning team, you have more pressure, naturally, because you're trying to finish in first place. Like Toe Blake told us, 'Second place for the Canadiens is as bad as last place for another team.' So you had the pressure of winning every game. You got in the play-offs, and you had to produce again to win the Cup. You were giving one hundred percent always since every team you met was keyed up to beat you. You were the best, and they played one hundred percent against you. If we knew that we had a key game coming up, we could give even more than that. That's why we stayed on top.

"But then I went to New York. We had a losing team. We didn't make the play-offs when I was there.

There is a different kind of pressure—from the fans, the newspapers—but it's pressure nevertheless. So it doesn't matter where you are. The pressure, it is always there."

Pressure. Constant. Day or night. Eight, nine months a year. It's why these men with the scarred stomachs and stitched smiles insist that nobody can truly understand a goaltender unless he is one.

What about the shots themselves? Does one particular player's shot cause a particular kind of pressure? Yes, according to Maniago, and his answer is somewhat surprising.

"I'm more afraid of Phil Esposito's shot than Dennis Hull's. Esposito's won't hurt me. It's not fast or hard enough. But Phil will embarrass me. He embarrasses me by scoring. Dennis will shoot bombs from all over, but Phil won't do anything unless he's in close. And that's where he can really hurt, really embarrass you. When Phil comes over the blue line, you don't know if he'll shoot, pass or come in deep with the puck. With Hull, you just know that as soon as he comes across the blue line, boom, you've got a shot. It's easier to stop, because you're ready for it."

Plante agrees that the hard slap shot is easier to stop, but he stresses the importance of being prepared both physically and mentally.

"After the play is in progress," he explains, "you have player changes. You have to keep track of who replaces who. He may be a good scorer. Maybe it's Bobby Hull who jumps on the ice. You might think it's just another player, someone who hasn't a prayer of beating you from fifty feet, but then the puck is coming, much harder than you expected, and it is in your net—all because you weren't prepared for Bobby Hull being out there.

"You have to mentally prepare yourself to face those guys with the hard shots. You have a book on everybody you're going to face—the kind of shot they have, whether they shoot high or low, where they shoot from and whether they go for your head or pass the puck if they have no angle. The lines also have different patterns. The Hadfield line, the Esposito line and the Mikita line have certain patterns they use when they come over the blue line. So you have to know where everybody goes and who can hurt you. If John Bucyk is on the ice, I'll know where he stands, how he gets the puck and what he does when he has it. You have to remember all these things."

The pressure that comes from waiting for a game to start is sometimes no more nerve-racking than wait-

"I know teams that start off by shooting from outside the blue line. I defy them, picking off everything. Then as the game progresses they're coming in closer, shooting from well inside the blue line, trying to work everything in front. That's all the better for me."

151

ing during a game. When a goalie's team is going strong, their opponents continually unable to clear the puck or muster an offense, a goalie stands alone, waiting for the action to come back to him. He may go seven minutes without making a save. Cesare Maniago, for one, doesn't like that.

"If, with a few minutes to go in a game, the score is tied or you're winning by one goal, what keeps going through my mind is, 'They're not going to get anything. They're not going to get anything.' If the action is down in the other end, those thoughts nag at you. You begin to tense. Believe me, it's better to be busy. When the action is at the other end, you fear a sudden two-on-one or a three-on-one break. Then you think, 'Oh, oh. Here they come.' You tighten more. You want to bear down more, but you get too tight. Then you shout to yourself, 'I'm relaxed! I'm relaxed!'

"But once they come into your zone, the thinking stops. You see the break and you think, 'Oh, oh. What am I going to do now?' Then they come over the line and make the play, and you go blank; instinct takes over. The play is in your zone. You don't have time to worry. You react. The hell with the pressure.

"It's analogous to what happens before a game. You're there. All you can do is dress and think. You break out in a cold sweat. You're anxious; you want to get the game going, because once the game starts you somehow feel at home. The first shot helps, and it's better if it comes early. If they don't get a shot until the six- or seven-minute mark, you're waiting and thinking, 'When? When?' "

The "big save" can do many things to a hockey game. It can instill instant confidence, not only in the goaltender who may suddenly feel invincible, but in his team as well. A well-timed kick-save on a breakaway may reverse a game's momentum. The team and its fans are revitalized, or the opponents begin to suspect that no matter what they do, they won't score. Possibly, they let down a little. However, a big save often goes unnoticed by all but the goaltender himself because it is not always a great save.

"There are moments out there during a game, when you just feel great," Dryden explains. "It's not always when you've made the spectacular save or stopped a breakaway. Take our last game in New York. A couple plays weren't necessarily dangerous plays, but I really could have played them badly. Rod Gilbert and Vic Hadfield were just off the corner of the net on the power play, and they really didn't have much of an angle. I could have gone out at them, but it would have been wrong, because they could have passed the puck behind me where it could have been ticked in. Instead I just sort of confronted them. I thought, 'OK, I don't have everything covered like I might have if I came out at you, but you don't have that much to shoot at either. You've still got to beat me, and you have a very difficult choice on your hands. Since you don't have that much to shoot at, you may want to pass—but that's your problem.'

"Rather than taking the decision away from the guy by coming out at him, I forced him, in this case, to pass. Nobody in Madison Square Garden noticed that. But it was something that gave me confidence, because I played it the way I did."

"All kinds of things can happen out there—good and bad," Plante adds. "If a goal is scored on you because you've had a lapse, you feel bad. You think about it. The play starts over again, it goes to the other end of the rink and you think about your lapse. You think, 'Well I was caught on the short side or on the long side, or I should have been out further to cut down the angle.' Or maybe you went out and passed the puck to the wrong man and it wound up in your net.

"While you think of these things, your mind is not in the game, and then, when they come back at you, you fight the puck. You protect the long side and leave the short side open. Or you flop on the ice because you had a goal scored along the ice, and then they shoot and hit the top of the net. It goes from bad to worse. You think about it from game to game. You continue to overcompensate. This is why a goaltender gets in a slump. In his own mind, he is trying to correct the mistake rather than just playing angles, playing his normal way."

A slump does bad things to a goaltender's average. And goalies think in terms of average. Permitting under three goals a game is considered outstanding work, but it's not easy, especially if you have a porous defense in front of you. It might not be your fault, but it shows in your average.

"There are times I wish I were a forward," Dryden laments. "Forwards are so lucky. All they have to do is skate and shoot, with virtually no other responsibilities. When they score a goal, it goes up there on the board. One goal for our side. You can't take that goal away from him—not tonight, not tomorrow, not next week. He's always got that goal. But with a goaltender, it's the goals-against average that counts.

Ex-Bruin Gerry Cheevers paints a new stitch on his
mask whenever he gets hit to remind him what
his face would look like if he played without a mask.

153

OK, so I get a shutout tonight. Great. But maybe tomorrow night I let in eight. Now my average is four, which is bad, even though I got a shutout. Now, in spite of that shutout, I've got to work extra hard just to bring my goals-against average down to below three."

With expansion bringing more games and more travel, most teams in the National Hockey League have gone to a two-goalie system. Gump Worsley and Cesare Maniago, teammates at Minnesota, have differing views on the benefits of expansion.

"There's pressure today, but it's nothing like it used to be," Worsley says. "At least not for me. Before expansion, there were six goaltenders in the NHL who played sixty-five or seventy odd games a year. They not only had the pressure of the job but the pressure of not doing badly for too long. There were ten or fifteen other goaltenders waiting around to take their jobs. *That* was pressure."

"When there were only six teams in the league, there was an abundance of goaltenders," repeats Maniago. "If I was second string in New York, Eddie Giacomin was playing most of the games. I was the backup goaltender. But I also knew that there were three or four goaltenders in the New York system capable of backing up Giacomin. It was the kind of situation where I felt, 'Am I really wanted?' Did they really expect as many things of me as, say, the fellow behind me? Did I figure in their plans? In those days they used to ship individuals in and out like cattle. There was no rationale to it whatsoever. I felt that they really didn't show the confidence toward me that they do now in expansion, when goaltenders aren't that easy to come by. As soon as I was drafted by Minnesota, I felt that I was needed by the team, that they were dependent upon me. In New York, they weren't. I wanted to play as well as I could in both places, yet I don't think they were as appreciative of me in New York as they are in Minnesota."

The relationship between a player and his coach, is extremely important but often tenuous. While almost every coach in the NHL was a player at one time, his attitudes can't jibe with those of every player on the squad. Less obvious, however, is the fact that of all the coaches, only one, Emile Francis of New York, was a goaltender. And of all the players most in need of understanding and help, the goaltenders must certainly head the list.

"A big problem today, as it has always been, is that the goaltenders don't talk enough with their coaches," says Plante. "A goaltender is worth between fifty and sixty-five percent of a game. It is important that he have a good relationship with his coach so that he can tell him how he feels. If he's hurt, or if he's having trouble on certain shots, then the coach can make some time available in practice when the goaltender can work on these mistakes. But most coaches don't know what a goaltender is going through.

"A coach should sit with his goalie and say, 'Look, I know you're having trouble with these shots. What can we do to help you?' If the coach and the goalie have a good relationship, it can help tremendously in winning more games. The goaltender's going to play better. He's going to feel wanted, rather than feel he's always doing something wrong and dragging down the team. Mistakes are part of the game, but the goaltender cannot afford mistakes."

"We're a breed of our own," continues Maniago. "I can take criticism, but only helpful criticism. If I have a coach who comes up to me and just reams me from the floor to the ceiling, I'll throw all the equipment in his face and say, 'Here, you go out and play the position.'

"Goaltenders don't need that. The job is tough enough without it. There's no way you're going to remedy a mistake by that sort of behavior. We all know the mistake that was made, and we all learn by our mistakes. A forward may not know he's not skating or scoring as well as he should. Most coaches can see that and explain it. The problem is that most coaches have never played in goal, and I think only a goaltender can tell a goaltender what his mistakes are. If I have a problem I'll go to Gump and say, 'Gump, I don't know what's going on. Am I backing in too soon, am I playing too deep, am I playing too far ahead of the goal? What am I doing wrong?' Then we'll both try to correct the mistakes I've been making.

"Emile Francis, just because he was a former goaltender himself, seems to be more sensitive to his goaltenders. I respected Emile. There were stories written about the misunderstanding between Emile and me. Emile's from the old school and I think I am too. In a game against Boston, there was a shot from the point that John MacKenzie deflected in front of the net. The puck came up and split my lip. You get these things all the time, and sometimes you bounce right back. But when I came back to the

bench after getting seven or eight stitches in my lip, Emile asked me how I felt and I said, 'Not too good.' I was just being truthful. Perhaps Emile wanted me to react a little differently.

"He said, 'OK. Fine.' Giacomin went in, and we lost in the last couple minutes. I don't know whether Emile was looking for a scapegoat or what, but he put the entire blame on me for the loss, because I had not gone back in. I think he felt that if I could walk to the bench, I could play. I felt bad enough about it, and I would have preferred to just drop the subject then and there.

"I do respect Emile, and he was really very helpful to me. It was just a misunderstanding."

"Goaltenders have their own language, there is no doubt about that," says Dryden. "But I haven't really talked to that many goaltenders yet. The two I've talked to most are my brother Dave, who's with the Buffalo Sabres, and, on this recent trip to Russia, Eddie Johnston of Boston. Mostly we talk about peripheral stuff, but also about physical problems and fear that you may be injured and can't play. You talk about a practice when somebody will come down and let a high, hard one go, and you'll go to the dressing room in disgust. And you and the other goaltender will be looking at each other and thinking, 'Now why would that man shoot like that?'

"The idea behind a goalie working hard in prac-

"You go into each game with a bit of uncertainty."
That uncertainty often increases when one plays
for an expansion team. Here, Gary Edwards misses.

tice—and I work hard in practice—is helping the
shooters as well as helping oneself. If he's working
then you should be working. If he's going to work
hard and go through the trouble of getting into a
scoring situation, then he should have you working
hard to keep him from scoring. If you're not, you're
doing him an injustice.

"But as far as I'm concerned, a guy is stupid to
go the length of the ice, wind up and let a slap shot
go from thirty feet. Anybody can play like that. It's
not going to happen in a game and all he's doing
is placing me in jeopardy. He's not using his head,
so forget it. I'm just going to be a little more careful
on somebody like that."

Other than the two-goalie system, a major
change for goaltenders in the last decade has been
the mask. Once nobody used one, then only Jacques
Plante now almost everybody. Today, most goaltenders can't understand a colleague who won't use
a mask. Dryden, a relative newcomer, is shocked to
think of it.

"You know," he says, "Eddie Johnston played
without a mask for many years, and it was only a very
serious injury in practice that required him to wear
one. I wonder what he would have done in the Parent
situation a couple years ago in New York, when
Bernie's mask was stolen with five minutes to go in
the game? Would Eddie have played that five minutes
without a mask? I wouldn't, and I don't think he would
have either."

"We were practicing in Detroit," Johnston recalls.
"Bobby Orr took a shot and I took my eyes off the
puck for a split second. I was wearing a mask but the
puck hit me above the mask, on the left side of the
head. I was in the hospital in Detroit for four days,
but after that I seemed all right, and the doctors said
I could go home to Boston. They didn't know that a
clot had formed near the brain. If the clot had moved
at all during that flight, I would have been dead.

"As it was, I got sick on the plane. I don't remember anything about the trip, but Ted Green picked
me up at the airport, and when I got off the plane he
hardly recognized me. The right side of my head was
swollen terribly.

"Greenie took me straight to the hospital. I was
there for eight weeks. People would come to see me,
but I don't remember what they said. They told me
that priests came, that my brother came, that I'd talk
to them and an hour later, I wouldn't even remember.
I lost forty or fifty pounds.

"Every morning for the first two weeks they took
me to the operating room. Most of the doctors wanted
to operate and get that clot out of there before it
moved and killed me. But that probably would have
meant the end of my career. One doctor insisted that
they wait, that the clot might go away. It finally did.

"When I came back to play I wore a heavy,
helmet-type mask. The first time I practiced I was
really worried. I was afraid I'd be gun-shy. I had to
find out. I make a living from being a goaltender, and
a goaltender can't be gun-shy, so I took that mask
off and told the guys to fire the puck right at me. Milt
[Schmidt, then the Boston general manager] saw me
take the mask off and came running down to the ice.

'You put that mask right back on, Eddie,' he yelled. 'You put that damn mask back on.' "

"There's no way I would ever play without a mask," Dryden insists. "Absolutely no way. I didn't start wearing one until I was forced to in college. Up to that point, masks weren't particularly fashionable. They hadn't been accepted by management either. Jacques Plante had difficulty convincing management that he should wear a mask. 'You have a bad game, it may be the mask, Jacques,' they'd say. 'Maybe you should get rid of it.'

"Or if it wasn't specifically stated, then it was sort of intimated that maybe you don't see the puck as well with a mask, that maybe you're afraid."

"Every goaltender is afraid that one time or another he is going to be hurt by a shot," says Plante, the man responsible for the mask. "You have Bobby Hull winding up thirty or forty feet away. Sometimes he shoots over the net, and naturally you're going to pull up on him. Depending on the angle he has, who is coming with him and the time he has to shoot, you're afraid of those shots. It's a natural fear. If you didn't have fear, you wouldn't be fighting for your life out there, you wouldn't be all keyed up, and you wouldn't play well. It's there, this fear, and you know it's part of the job. You know you don't like it, but you have to live with it. If you don't fight the fear then you start shying away from the shots, and a lot

157

of bad goals are going to be scored on you right along the ice. When you're afraid, you lift your shoulders and your stick leaves the ice.

"In the days when there wasn't the mask I didn't think about it. I took it for granted that there was no mask for the goaltenders, and I played just like everybody else. But at that time, you didn't have too many slap shots. The slap shot came in about 1950 or the late forties, and maybe you had one player per team who had a really good slap shot, and he was the one that you looked for. You still look for the hardest shots, because they can score on you from the blue line. They can make you look bad, or if you're not very, very careful, they'll catch you in the back of your net and score. These days, you stop the puck with whatever you can get in front of it, not what you want to get in front of it. So as for the mask, it's there now, and I wouldn't think about playing without it. That would be ridiculous.

"I remember playing in New York when Bernie Parent lost his mask with five minutes to go in the game. He threw his mask into the stands during a disturbance, and the fans kept it. The coach asked him if he wanted to finish the game, and Bernie said no. So I had to finish it. There is no way that Bernie will go out there without a mask, and I'm the same way. It's like asking a baseball catcher, 'You have only one inning to go. Want to catch without a mask?'

"But you still have goaltenders that go out there without a mask. Like Gumper. The reason is he never had a broken bone in his face. If he got a good shot that broke his cheekbone, his nose or jaw, then he would think twice. The mask is there. It's available. It's accepted. Use it.

"Besides that, hockey's your bread and butter. If you lose an eye, that's it. You get hit in the face, you start to be afraid of the puck and your career is over. Another thing: You don't die after hockey. If you lose an eye and your career is over, you have to live the rest of your life with one eye."

"Jacques has said that he'll keep playing hockey until I wear a mask," Worsley states. "Well, he'll be playing until he's eighty. Jacques has a company that manufactures masks. Maybe he wants to sell me one.

"I don't wear a mask because I don't like them. Wearing a mask isn't easy. It takes a long time to get used to, and after twenty years it's a little late to start. It would take two years to get used to it, and

I'm sure my work would suffer. So I just grin and bear it, ha, ha. Besides, Cesare caught one in the mouth last year with a mask on and got seven stitches. If he hadn't had a mask on, he'd have gotten fourteen stitches. The difference is seven stitches. That's not enough to make me wear a mask.

"I'm not afraid of getting hurt. I expect it. If you're going to be out there worrying that the puck's going to hit you in the face, it'll hit your net instead. I'll stop the puck with my face if I have to. I don't want to, but it's better than having the puck in my net.

"The toughest thing to handle in the games are the screen shots. You've got to keep your eye on that puck. When it's in the corner and they send it back out to the point, guys are always crowding around you, trying to screen you and deflect the shot up, down, sideways, any way they can. You can't look over them, so you've got to crouch down and try to see through their legs. To do that you've got to stick your nose right down along that ice and try to keep track of the puck. It's harder when you're wearing a mask.

"I've been hit in the face many times. Once, during a game with Toronto, Garry Monahan took a shot that I went to my knees to block. The puck hit my pads and rebounded right out to Jim Harrison, who let fly a wicked shot that I'm still looking for. It hit me flush on the nose and down I went, like I'd been shot. Somebody told me later that after I hit the ice, my arms and legs were still moving, like a kid making angels in the snow. I said that comes from experience; after twenty years in the NHL you'll kick out a rebound even when you're unconscious.

"I have to admit, though, I've been lucky. I've never had any serious injuries. A lot of cuts but no broken bones. I've still got a few lumps on my nose from Harrison's shot, so maybe my nose was broken, I don't know. Guys like Eddie Johnston, Johnny Bower and Roger Crozier have all been injured quite seriously, so I understand why they might go to the mask.

"I've been hit a number of times by Bobby Hull's shots, but again I've been very lucky. When Hull winds up and lets fly, that puck comes at you like a small town. That puck comes so fast that I've never been able to figure out how it has time to turn over before it gets to you. But Bobby's shots that hit me somehow hit me flat, and when the puck hits you flat it'll stun you, maybe cut you, even knock you out, like it did me. But for some reason the puck is more dangerous

when it hits you straight on. Then, it's like a sabre. It has a cutting edge. Maybe it's something like the difference between slapping someone in the face and hitting him with your fist.

"Of course, when the puck hits you in the face it hurts a little more than a fist."

"You know, as a kid, it's almost like a real badge to have a little cut," Dryden notes, "and as a kid, that's all you get—a little cut or a black eye. You go to school the next day, and you're sort of the tough kid. But then, after a while, the bloody thing starts hurting too much. If you're ten, twelve, fourteen years old, the puck just isn't coming that hard. Then you're fifteen, sixteen, seventeen, and the puck starts really moving, and they're not little cuts anymore. They really hurt. There's the potential of a very serious injury. You weigh the status of the badge of courage versus all that pain. Then it's just not worth it anymore. So I started to wear a mask and have never gone without it for a moment since. It's absolutely a part of me now. Fortunately, it's accepted as a part of your equipment. Now there's just no way. . . .

"I feel very uncomfortable playing against goalies who don't wear masks. Like Gumper. He's going down

in a scramble, and I'll say to myself, 'Gump, get up!' I sort of hope Gump gets, well, just a minor one, an easy one, off the cheek, and he'll say, 'That's it, I'm wearing a mask from now on.' But he won't."

"It's nice to hear Kenny say something like that," Maniago states. "He's really being sympathetic toward Gump. I'm the same way. I more or less tried to convince Gump that if he's not going to wear a mask in the game, at least wear it in practice. I mean, what is a practice? Nothing's really at stake. But as they say, you can't teach an old dog new tricks. He's a stubborn fellow, and he's not going to change his ways. Yet when he's out there playing and I'm on the bench, I'm always fearful that he might get hurt. I'm sure he's thinking, 'Stitch or two, that's nothing.'

"A broken cheekbone led me to wearing a mask. It was in a game against Philadelphia. It was in that year that the roof blew off the Spectrum, and the Flyers had to play the remainder of their games in Quebec City. The lighting wasn't too good there. Somebody took a rising shot from about ten feet. I kind of turned my head to avoid the shot, and it caught me in the side of the face and broke my cheekbone. That really led me to wear the mask,

"With players using curved sticks, you just don't know what the puck is going to do." *Above:* Hadfield blasts away at Binkley. *Left:* Giacomin juggles loose puck.

because more and more goalies were starting to do it at the time. I felt, heck, if I was going to play this game any longer, I'd better go out and find some sort of facial protection I felt comfortable with."

Mask or no mask, goaltenders are constantly injured. Usually their injuries are more serious than those of other players. They're constantly diving on the ice, falling against the steel pipes of the cage, sticking their heads into a fray of swinging sticks from which a puck can suddenly come flying at lethally high speed. It's a tribute to their courage that they keep playing.

"I have had two concussions in my life," Plante explains. "One was against Boston, when Vic Stasiuk was pushed into me with his stick up. He gave me a cross-check that broke my nose. As I fell back, I hit my head on the crossbar and got a concussion. But

this one wasn't as severe as the one in St. Louis. I only went to the hospital for three days.

"In St. Louis, during the play-off finals in 1970, I really don't know what happened. I remember being hit and that's it. I could see Fred Stanfield wind up at the blue line, and I had a clear path to the puck. The puck was coming, oh, about an inch from the ice, and I bent down to catch it. The first thing I knew I was knocked out. I don't recall seeing Esposito in front, but apparently he deflected the puck between my eyes.

"When I woke up, they told me I would have to go to the dressing room. I said, 'Fine, I'll take five minutes and then come back.' But the doctor didn't see it that way. He said, 'We'll take you to the hospital and if you're all right, then you can play the next game.'

"When I got in the hospital they moved me from

the stretcher to the X-ray machine and back to the stretcher again—four times. I wasn't supposed to be moved that much. The fourth time, they wanted me to get up and go for more X rays, I started to throw up. Dr. Probstein, who was with the intern who was taking the X rays, said I could have died right there. He told me that without the mask, I would have been dead.

"Every time I see the replay of that shot, I can feel the pain. I've never had so much pain in my life. When I was knocked out, I didn't feel anything but when I was in the hospital, just moving my eyes sideways made me throw up. I've never felt pain like that before. I wouldn't wish that on anybody.

"When you hear that another goalie has been hurt, you just hope that it's not serious. But until it touches you, you really don't know what's happening. Injury is part of the game. The guys get hurt and you say, 'Well, let's hope that it's not serious,' but it doesn't really touch you to the point where you say, 'I'm going to quit because it could happen to me.' You don't think about those things.

"Goaltenders, you see, don't like to admit they're afraid. A goaltender is afraid, but you can't notice it often. But watch in the practices. When somebody winds up, the goalie's stick comes up, the catching glove moves up and the guy is backing into the net, instead of just digging in. It's just like that in baseball; a hitter will dig in, and they brush him off. Then they'll throw him a curve, and he'll just kind of swipe at it.

"Those hard shooters, they'll come in and slap that puck, and you've just got to lift on it. You know that it's dangerous. You know that if it hits your arm, it's going to hurt, and that the pain will be there a long time. The arms are bony, and a bone bruise hurts for a lot of games. If you get hurt on the stick side, well, that's it. You can't hold the stick. You're paralyzed. You get hit on the catching side, and the next time someone winds up, you're afraid to stick that glove out there."

Ken Dryden fights his fear aggressively. He likes to think he initiates action rather than reacts to it. He goes out *at* the shots and dismisses the thought that he is only a target, a mere extension of the cage.

"If you sit back and logically think about the fact that you're guarding something," he explains, "and you get beaten—just once—well, you think you haven't done your job, in spite of the fact that you have done it if you've only let in two or three.

"You've got to maintain this perspective, and I

Jean Ratelle works the puck in close against Detroit's Andy Brown, but Brown makes the initial stop and gives Ratelle little chance to score off the rebound.

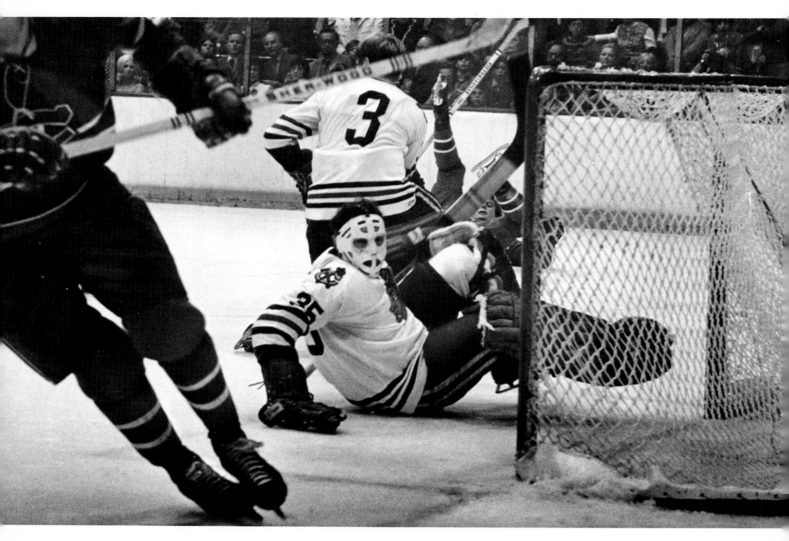

Jacques Plante was the first goaltender to move out of the goal area.
Tony Esposito, 35, plays similarly, flopping unceremoniously
to make a save or occasionally moving to the boards *(following pages)*.

think most goaltenders, in their own way, are actually much more aggressive than passive. A shot very rarely hurts if you stop it, but if *it* hits *you,* it hurts. If it hits you, it suggests that you're not ready for it. Then it really hurts. But when you're actually moving into a shot, when you're prepared, it never hurts.''

"I'll study goaltenders and notice that there are some that do stand motionless, like they are the target,'' muses Maniago. "Then the other club says, 'OK, let's fire on him.' Whereas the goalies who are a little more aggressive, who challenge the shooters, who defy them, find the opposition will tend to try to work the puck in a little closer and finesse a goal, rather than taking the long shot.

"It's all mental, of course. I know teams that start off by shooting from outside the blue line. I defy them, picking off everything. Then as the game progresses they're coming in closer, shooting from well inside the blue line, and before you know it, they're trying to work everything in front. That's all the better for me. The more passing plays they have, the more problems they're going to have. They're increasing the chances of your teammates breaking up the play. The name of this game is shooting.''

If shooting is the name of the game, then the best shooters will score the most goals. According to Worsley and the record books, the theory holds true.

"I've played nineteen years here,'' says Worsley, "and I'd have to say that Bobby Hull, Gordie Howe and Bernie Geoffrion had the best shots. Geoffrion was one of those guys who could really blast it—that's why they called him the Boomer. He was also one of those guys who didn't know where it was going. The puck might take off and land thirty rows back in the seats, or it could be right along the ice. You just never knew.

"It was sort of the same thing with Howe, except that *you* never knew where the puck was going, but Gordie usually did. Gordie very seldom used the slap shot. You never knew when he was going to shoot. No warning. Here it comes. Were you ready? Too bad. Fish it out of the net.''

"Howe had a good slap shot,'' Plante agrees, "but he rarely used it, and then, usually when he was alone. Or he might use it when he was on a bad angle. Howe always had this little snap. He very seldom laid into the puck. But he was a master at putting the puck where you were not.

"Howe had a heavy shot, others have light shots.

It's all in the way you hit the puck. Some guys put more beef into it, and with others it's just a little snap. Our Paul Henderson has a great shot, but it's a light shot. It's a quick motion, just a snap. Bobby Orr has a heavy shot. It comes in, you catch it and it feels like lead. It can knock you off balance if you're not ready for it, and if you're not careful, it can leave somebody like Phil Esposito with a great rebound.''

"Bobby Hull's got a big shot, but it isn't a wild shot,'' Maniago says. "Take his brother Dennis for instance. I'd say Dennis has every bit as hard a shot as Bobby, but he was never as accurate as Bobby. Possibly you are a little more fearful of Dennis, because an odd shot is coming at your head. With Bobby you knew that most of the time the puck was going to be on net.

"Now with Phil Esposito, it is not a case of a hard shot at all. Phil's main asset is converting a pass into a shot all in one motion, and accurately. He's an artist at deflecting shots, and he's great at anticipating how much time he has to deke a goaltender. In these three categories nobody else in the league can come close to Phil. That's why he scored seventy-six goals in a year. But from the blue line, there are thirty guys who have harder shots.''

Despite all the stories about Howe's meanness, he probably never hurt another player unless he felt that the guy deserved it, or that it was necessary for self-preservation.

"I'll never forget the time we were playing Detroit when I was with the Rangers,'' says Worsley. "I managed to block a shot by sprawling on my belly, and the puck went out to Howe, who was standing about five feet away. It was right on his stick. If he wanted to he could have just flicked his wrists and put both the puck and my head in the net. But Gordie just shoved the puck under my body. There was a whistle, and as I got up I said, 'Thanks, you'll get it next time.' He didn't say anything, but he looked at me as if to say, 'Don't worry. I know I will.'

"Bobby Hull was the same kind of a guy. Once I got knocked out by one of his shots. When I woke up in the dressing room, there was Bobby, looking down at me. He no more wanted to see me hurt than I did.

"Bobby liked to swing wide as he came in on the left side, and usually he fired away at the far side of the net—the goalie's left side. You knew he'd do that most of the time, and I often cheated to that side, not

that it helped me that much. With Howe, though, you couldn't ever cheat. If he caught you leaning, before you knew it the puck would be in the net."

"The game is so much different now," says Plante. "In the 1950s, they used to carry the puck in and try to work it in close. The shots were slower and not as hard. Only a few players used the slap shot. But now they either dump the puck in our end and chase it, or else they come across the blue line and just blast away at you. With players like Hull, Mikita, Hadfield and Gilbert using curved sticks, you just don't know what the puck is going to do. It might dip, it might sail. You just never know."

"Some people think they put in the rule that a stick can only have a one-inch curvature to protect the goaltenders," Worsley reflects. "I think they did it because so many shots were taking off and hitting people in the stands."

Like his roommate, Maniago has been the victim of his share of milestone goals. He was in goal for New York when Geoffrion got his 50th goal, and when Bobby Hull scored his 51st. "I was also playing one night in Detroit when Howe and Alex Delvecchio both set records on the same goal," he recalls. And for Minnesota, Maniago has been in the nets for two crushing goals by the St. Louis Blues—Ron Schock's breakaway score that won the seventh game in double overtime of the Stanley Cup quarterfinals in 1968, and Kevin O'Shea's overtime goal that won the seventh game of the 1972 quarterfinals. On O'Shea's shot, from about 35 feet out on right wing, the puck flew over Maniago's right shoulder, struck the goalpost and caromed off the goaltender's stick handle into the net!

"Those were heartbreaking goals," he admits, "and maybe a few years ago I couldn't have swallowed it. But I've sort of changed things in my own mind as far as pressures are concerned. I've learned, through experience, that I must shrug things off. If I don't, I'm finished. I suffer after the game and possibly the next day. But before, it used to bother me for days and days. I don't let that happen to me now. What's behind me is past. I think of the present and the future, not the past."

Goaltenders do have their high moments. Ask Ken Dryden, who helped engineer one of the biggest upsets in sports history when the Montreal Canadiens deflated the mighty Boston Bruins in the quarterfinals of the 1971 Stanley Cup play-offs. In the days preceding the series, there was talk of a four-game sweep

for the Bruins. The Bruins, with Phil Esposito and Bobby Orr leading the way, had run away with the East Division title of the NHL with 121 points. Montreal had finished a distant third with 97. Setting an all-time record of 399 goals, the Bruins had nine players with more than 20 goals, five with more than 30, three with more than 40, two with more than 50 and Esposito with an incredible total of 76.

The Canadiens answered with an unproven goaltender who had been hauled out of the American League to play six games near the end of the season. When the Bruins won the first game of the series, 3–1, and broke into a 5–1 lead in the second, the crowd in Boston Garden sensed a sweep. But something happened—the Bruins have yet to figure out what. The Canadiens roared back to win that second game, 7–5, and with Dryden robbing Bruin gunners right and left, managed to split the next four games. During one stretch, the young goaltender went 90 minutes without allowing the Bruins a goal. In the seventh and deciding game, Dryden was once again a sensation. The Canadiens won the game and the series, 4–2.

Montreal then defeated Minnesota in six games and won the Stanley Cup in a seven-game series against Chicago.

"That Boston series was a bad situation," Dryden recalls, "but at the same time it was almost a perfect situation to have happen early in my career.

"I'm glad I didn't play against Boston toward the end of the season. It would have been too discouraging. They were handling us. We were in third place, going nowhere, and the games didn't really mean that much to us. It reflected in our play, and Boston really bombed us. To play in a game like that would have been tough.

"Most of my experience with Boston had been on television. You're impressed—obviously you're impressed. You're impressed by the fact that they scored three-hundred-ninety-nine goals. You think, 'Wow, Boston scored eight again last night.' But it has not personally touched you. It's happened to someone else. As a result, you really don't know how good they are.

"So I think that I was going into the series with an open mind, partially. It was a tremendous feeling of elation, winning that series. That, and our comeback in Russia will always rank among the greatest thrills of my life.

"As they say, an experience like that is worth waiting for." Apparently it is, since it's hard to come up with any other reason for being a goaltender.

"My prime job is to keep our team ahead, even or no more than one goal behind at the end of the first period." Pittsburgh goalie Jim Rutherford applies the Dryden philosophy.

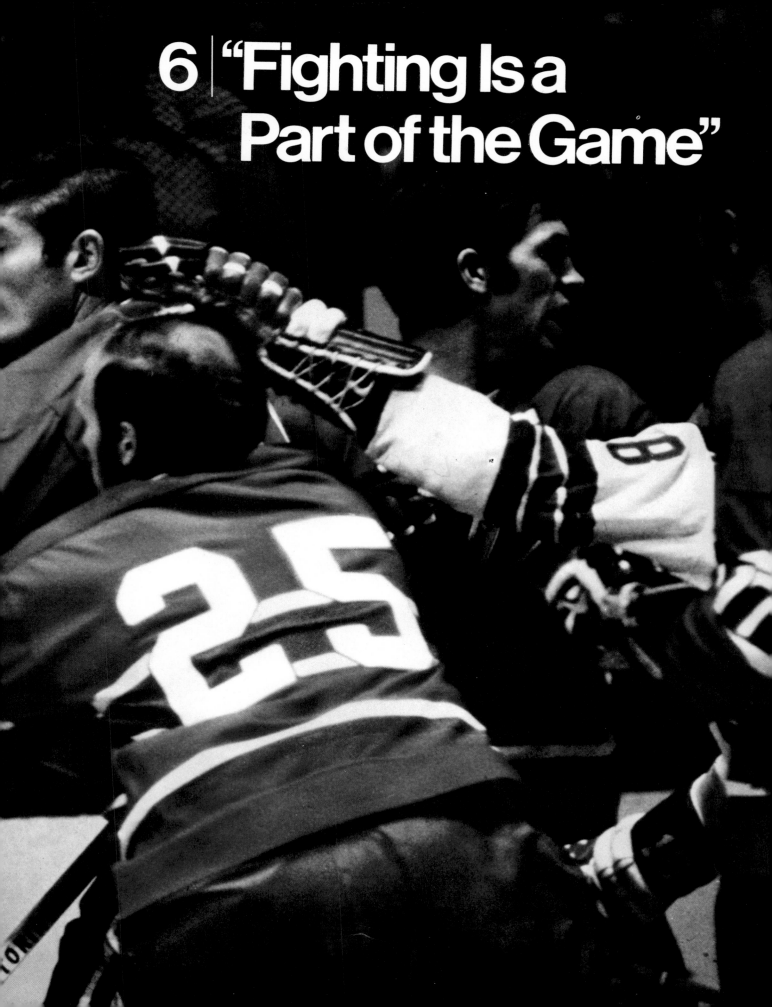

6 | "Fighting Is a Part of the Game"

Appropriately, they came together at the mecca of boxing —the old Madison Square Garden, at 50th Street and Eighth Avenue, where names such as Dempsey, Louis and Robinson had appeared on the marquee. But on this cold February night in 1959, there would be no boxing match. The marquee read RANGERS v. DETROIT, and what developed was a fistfight—gloves down, heads up—the unadorned champion against the unconvinced and willing challenger.

"The puck had gone into the corner," recalls Frank Udvari, the referee. "[Gordie] Howe had collided with [Eddie] Shack behind the net and lost his balance. He was just getting to his feet when here's [Lou] Fontinato at my elbow, trying to get at him.

"'I want him, I want him,' he said.

"'Leave him alone. Use your head,' I answered.

"'I want him.'

"'Be my guest,' I said."

With that, New York's fearsome Lou Fontinato charged Detroit's Gordie Howe, another heavyweight, whose physical and fistic prowess was a source of great respect around the league. Catching a glimpse of the imminent danger through the corner of his eye, Howe grabbed Fontinato's sweater at the neck and drove a right hand into his face.

"Never in my life had I heard anything like it, except maybe the sound of someone chopping wood," says Udvari. "*Thwack!* And all of a sudden Louie's breathing out of his cheekbone."

For all its speed and flair, its poetic grace and beauty, hockey is rooted in violence. Everything else being equal, the meanest team wins. Therefore all teams want at least one player who deals in punishment instead of points, who merely by stepping on the ice can introduce hesitation and perhaps even fear in the opposition. In addition to the rest of his unquestioned skills, Gordie Howe was such a player. So was Lou Fontinato, and their bitter confrontation has become the most famous in the game's history, brief and one-sided though it was. In return for a dislocated finger on his right hand and a gash above the eye, Howe furnished Fontinato with a broken nose, a fractured cheekbone and a substantial loss of teeth. Indeed, plastic surgery was ultimately required to reconstruct Fontinato's battered face, which was featured in a full-page spread in *Life* magazine.

Preceding pages: Good guys Ratelle, Mahovlich and Lemaire turn bad. *Right:* Former Ranger Syl Apps dishes it out to present Ranger Vic Hadfield.

Policemen or enforcers, thugs or hatchet men. Call them what you like, they are the bad guys. Either you love them or you hate them. Guys like Howe and Fontinato, Eddie Shore and Bill Ezinicki were bad guys. So were Ted Lindsay, Howie Young and Reggie Fleming. Some contemporary bad guys are Keith Magnuson and Bryan Watson, Orland Kurtenbach and Jim Dorey, Derek Sanderson and the brothers Plager—Bob, Barclay and Bill.

No player until Howe had been quite as bad as John Bowie Ferguson of Montreal. Before he retired to the serenity of a prospering men's sweater business in 1971, Ferguson was not only bad, he was cruel —a rock-hard 185-pounder who always got in the first punch and usually the last and whose victims invariably left the ice with blood streaming into a white towel. "I never could figure out why they bled so much," Ferguson says. "I guess it was my knuckles. I always had big, lumpy knuckles."

Ferguson despised the opposition. He refused to associate with them during the off-season and squirmed uncomfortably when forced to share a table with them at a banquet. "How can you chase a golf ball with somebody in the summer and then try to knock his head off in the winter?" he asked. "Some players say they can, but I doubt it. I know I can't."

Ferguson's only exceptions were defenseman Bryan Watson and goalie Les Binkley of the Pittsburgh Penguins. Ferguson was, and still is, a close friend of both, but that didn't keep him from plowing Binkley's head against a goalpost for 13 stitches one night or from trading elbows, high sticks and flying fists with Watson. At 170 pounds, Watson is a lightweight among NHL heavies, and his face—a crazy quilt of scars and stitches—shows it. Having fought most of the bad guys in the league despite his size, Watson's opinion has merit. "Nobody fights like Fergy," he says. "Nobody. Fighting was a way of life with Fergy. He showed no mercy."

"Where I came from," says Ferguson, "I learned to take nothing without giving a receipt."

Indeed, less than a minute into his first NHL game in 1963, rookie John Ferguson began thrashing Ted Green, former Boston strongboy and a league-leader in meanness. Five years later, Green sought a rematch, in an effort to inspire a band of young, wide-eyed Bruins who had just made the play-offs for the first time. Ferguson obliged by jerking Green's sweater over his head and pummeling him for a solid minute before the officials intervened. With its commander

Left: Fighter Orland Kurtenbach is squeezed out by Kings' Curtis and Harper. *Below:* Nonfighter Balon swings at Widing. *Bottom:* Tannahill cools it.

175

Defensemen, generally bigger than forwards, are more often the enforcers. *Above:* "The Chief," Jim Neilson, glowers with disdain. *Opposite top:* Keith Magnuson, one of the league's toughest. *Opposite bottom:* Bill White and stitched-together lip.

out of combat, the Bruins surrendered in four straight games.

Ferguson's most noted victory, however, came the night he knocked Eric ("Elbows") Nesterenko cold with one punch and hit him with another before Nesterenko reached the ice.

John Ferguson looked like the prizefighter he probably could have been. His face was pale and taut, and he looked at you with cold, hard eyes, deeply set in the skull. He had a hawk's nose. "My shield and buckler," Fergy jokingly called it. "It's done such a great job of guarding my face that I've still got my own teeth."

But, like prizefighters—and most of hockey's bad guys—Ferguson was a good guy off the ice; with few exceptions, a perfect gentleman and host, soft-spoken but articulate, a family man, who enjoyed his children. Typically, he still takes great pride in the fact that whenever battle was imminent, he had always been among the first to drop his stick. "Fighting is part of the game," he says. "It always will be. But the most important thing in a hockey fight is to get rid of your stick. A punch in the nose never hurt anyone seriously, but a swinging stick is another matter. Just look what happened to Green."

Edward Joseph ("Ted") Green—Terrible Teddy. Mean. At 5 feet 10 inches and 200 pounds, Green looked like a contract killer—black hair, dark and narrow eyes, heavy brows, bold cheekbones. And Terrible Teddy could stare. . . .

"Greenie had this way of staring at you," recalls Derek Sanderson with a shiver. "Just a long, cold, hard, deep stare. He didn't have to say a word. You just knew he was one, tough sonofabitch."

Although he never led the league in penalty minutes, Green was rarely far off the pace. And 10 years of cowing practically everyone in the NHL had its effect. The opposition always knew where Green was and what he was doing on the ice. Green liked it that way. Once his bad rep was firmly established, Green could concentrate on the more refined aspects of defensive play, to such an extent that he was voted to the All-Star team in the spring of 1969. That was also the year of the "accident."

On the night of September 21, 1969, Boston was playing an exhibition game against the St. Louis Blues in Ottawa. Thanks to Green, the Bruins of Orr, Esposito & Company were very rapidly becoming the meanest —and best—team in the NHL. After years of futility, Boston had risen to second place and lost out in the

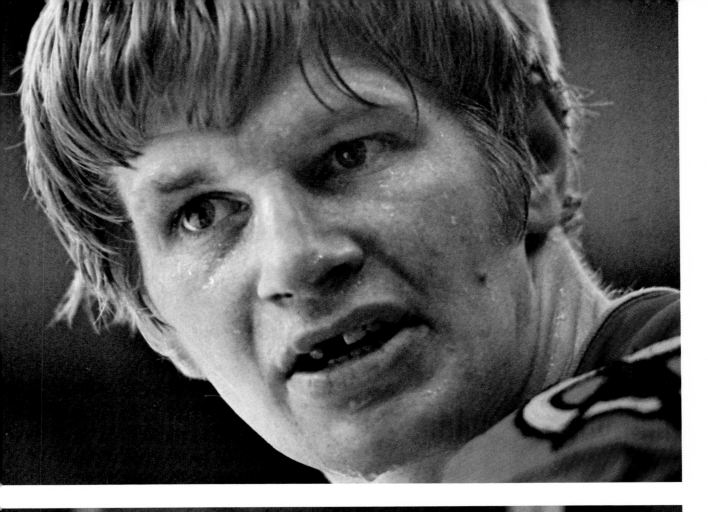

Below: Rookie Jim Schoenfeld of Buffalo poises his 200 pounds and evil-eyes the opposition. *Right:* Keith Magnuson is decked by 6-foot 5-inch Mahovlich.

play-offs only after a stirring, six-game series with Montreal, which went on to win the Stanley Cup in a four-game sweep of St. Louis. Now, on this warm night in Ottawa, the Bruins were preparing for what they expected would be their best year.

About 13 minutes were gone in a dull first period when the puck caromed behind the Boston net. Green went after it along with Wayne Maki, a young forward trying to make the St. Louis club. In the ensuing scuffle, Maki grabbed the back of Green's sweater. Annoyed, Green shoved a glove into Maki's face. Riled, Maki jabbed his stick into Green's abdomen. Incensed, Green chopped his stick on Maki's shoulder. Frightened, Maki swung back—the heel of his stick thudding against the right side of Green's head. Green sank to the ice, his head twisting violently, saliva seeping from the side of his mouth. Blood began oozing from a cut near his temple.

Green was rushed to the hospital, where it was determined that the left side of his body had been paralyzed by skull fragments driven through the tough membrane encasing the brain. With Green's life in the balance, doctors performed three delicate operations in the following months. They inserted a plate in his skull and strongly hinted that he would never play hockey again. Anyone but Terrible Teddy probably

wouldn't have returned. But a year later, following a strenuous rehabilitation program, Green was back with the Bruins—wearing a protective black helmet that ominously resembled an executioner's hood.

Without Green, the Bruins had finished second again and gone on to win their first Stanley Cup in 29 years. "But as hard as we tried, we couldn't be ourselves," said Bobby Orr. "We could still see Greenie lying there on the ice in Ottawa. Then one day—I guess it was about halfway through the season—Greenie came back to Boston for a press conference. We were down for practice, and without saying a word Greenie walked into the locker room. His head was shaved from the operations and everything, but he sat down where he used to sit and started putting on some underwear. As each of the guys came in, he'd give them a shot. He'd swear at them or something, just like the old Greenie. It was as if things were the way they used to be. We were all right after that."

But Green was not all right. He had trouble doing things on the ice that used to come automatically. He was no longer Terrible Teddy, the enforcer; opposing players virtually refused to become embroiled with him. When the Boston management decided against protecting him in the 1972 draft, Green signed a long-term contract with the WHA New England Whalers.

179

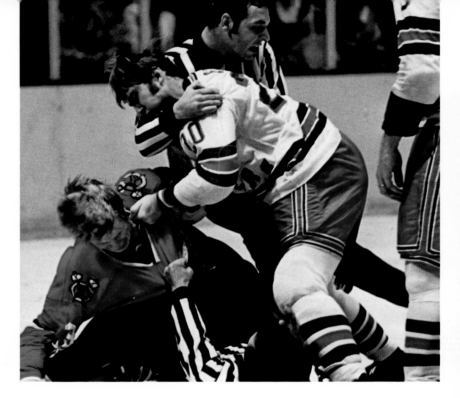

Top: Magnuson and Egers rough up a referee. *Above:*
Scrappy Glen Sather wears his badge of courage.
Right: ''The Spark,'' St. Louis's dogged Barclay Plager.

Above: Near-toothless mouth attests to the fact that Vic Hadfield is New York's enforcer. *Opposite:* Terry Harper throws his 197 pounds at Steve Vickers.

It is said that those who live by the sword shall die by the sword, and the fact that a player as tough and seemingly invincible as Ted Green almost died from a swinging stick had a sobering effect on professional hockey. Combatants thought twice before seeking to cut each other's heart out.

The feeling was nothing new to Howie Young, however. For years Young had lived with the fear that he might kill someone in a hockey game. "But that was when I was a drunk," Young says. "Nobody's human when he's drunk." Indeed, from New Westminster to Chicoutimi, from Rochester to Edmonton and most of the stops between, Howie Young was the consummate bad guy, a marauder who would take his stick to you as soon as look at you—and laugh about it afterward. In 1958–59, Young led the Quebec Hockey League in penalty minutes; in 1962–63 with Detroit, he set a National Hockey League record for most penalty minutes. Following a stint with Chicago, Young was banished to the old Los Angeles Blades of the Western Hockey League, which he led in penalty minutes in 1964–65 and 1965–66. "People would ask me about my penalty time," Young recalls. "All I can say is that when you're hung over, it isn't easy to keep up with a hockey game. I had to resort to other tricks."

But unlike the hawk-nosed Ferguson and the thuglike Green, Young had a following everywhere he played. Women fans in particular saw him as a tragic character who, in spite of his bloodcurdling escapades on the ice, seemed to need love and understanding more than a sound whipping from the local enforcer. And Young certainly didn't look like a bad guy; the gray eyes, straight white teeth and gleaming hair that swept along the sides of his head provided the appeal of a movie star. Young even had a part in the movie *None But the Brave,* produced and directed by Frank Sinatra. "They wanted somebody to play a drunk marine," Young recalls. "Frank told me just to be myself."

Those were the years when Young staggered through the nights and slept away the days; years of fights and arrests, of jail, suspensions and fines. Awakening in the late afternoon and facing a game that night, Young would stumble to the bathroom, shower, shave and dress. Then, often without pausing to eat, he would stagger into the back seat of a taxi for the ride to Chicago Stadium. As the cab moved along Madison Avenue, Young would peer out at the bums and winos, sprawled in the cold outside the

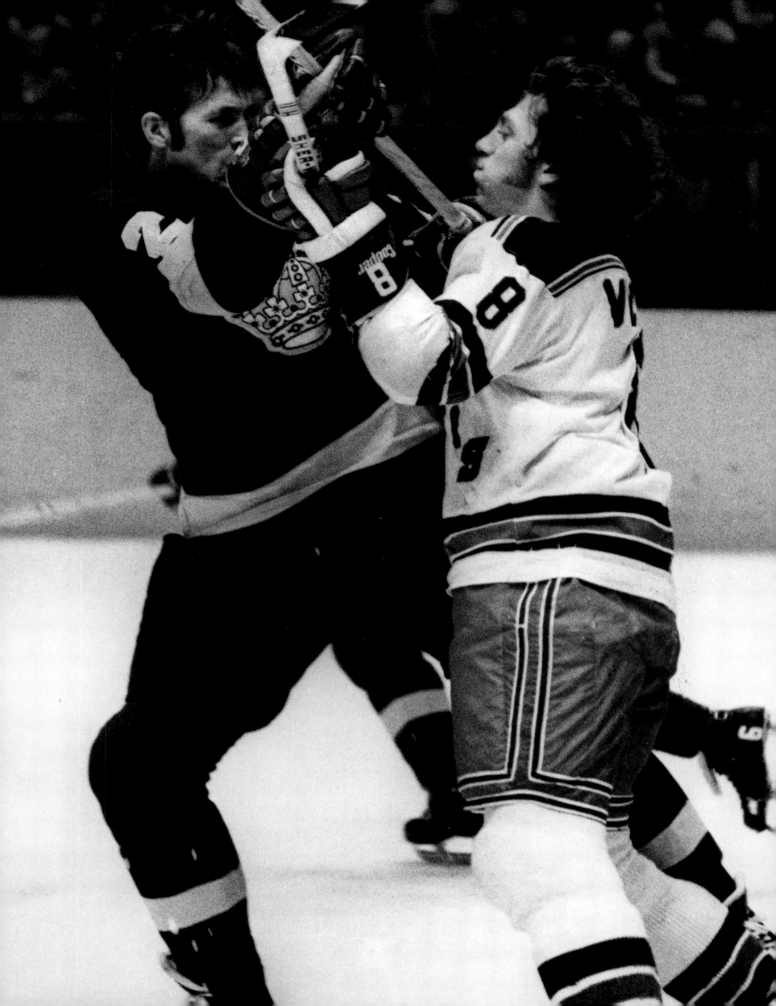

Opposite: Rambunctious ex-Bruin John McKenzie, better known as "Pie." *Left:* Rejean Houle gets up slowly after a hard check. *Below:* Rangers' Ted Irvine, acquired for his muscle, muscles Canadiens' Pierre Bouchard.

saloons. With their tattered coats and trousers, they looked like heaps of rags, in the glare of a blue-yellow neon beer sign. "I had myself convinced for some reason that I was different from them," Young recalls. "But there I was, proud as hell, going to the stadium just to make enough money to go out and get drunk again myself."

On many occasions Young simply didn't make it to the games, or to the train or plane taking his club to another city. Whenever he did play, his face turned a darker shade of crimson with every shift on the ice, while inside his head, he recalls, he felt as if a time bomb were ticking.

"I was sick," says Young. "And playing a game like hockey? With a *stick* in my hands? That stick might as well have been an extension of my arm, the way I used it in those days. I lived in constant fear that someday I was going to murder someone with that stick."

He came close. Once, when he was with the Red Wings, Young creased Ralph Backstrom's head in a game at Detroit. Blood pouring from the wound, Backstrom sank to the ice, unconscious. "I could have hit him harder if I'd wanted to," Young elaborated later.

Another time Young stormed 35 feet to run down Toronto goalie Johnny Bower like a rodent in the street. Bower was out for the rest of the season with a concussion and a dislocated shoulder.

Later that year, in the play-offs against Chicago, the Black Hawks' Murray Balfour burst past Detroit's Young and raced in on goal—a clear breakaway. Desperately, Young reached out with his stick and tripped him, sending Balfour careening into a goalpost. Like Bower, Balfour suffered a concussion and a dislocated shoulder. Before the same series was over, Young had also sent Stan Mikita hobbling from the ice on one leg.

"Something like the Balfour incident would just push me into a bar," Young recalls. "I'd remember the crowd, all twenty thousand of them, calling for my blood. Why, it was as if I was a Roman gladiator and they were turning their thumbs down on me. But then I'd get in that bar and have a few drinks, and pretty soon I'd feel special all over again. So special that I couldn't have done anything wrong. The world was all wrong and I was right. I'd have my ego back again.

"But then I'd be standing there at the bar, the lights down low and the soft music playing in the background, and a hooker might come over and strike up a conversation. I'd just start feeling superior to her when she'd say, 'Howie, why do you drink so much?' And there would go my ego out the window. That question probably drove me to more drinks than anything else."

The turning point in Howie Young's life came in May 1965, when he was bailed out of the drunk tank in downtown Los Angeles and somehow stumbled into a meeting of Alcoholics Anonymous. Young will never forget that day—May 5—because he hasn't had a drink since. Not a drop.

Drier and 20 pounds lighter, Young improved his play remarkably the following winter. For the first time in his career he played like the defenseman so many had expected him to be. However, Young's evangelical preaching on the evils of alcohol had begun to unnerve his teammates. Then, in a game about halfway through the season, Young drew a minor penalty for tripping. Instead of heading for the penalty box, he skated over to the man he had tripped and whacked him on the seat of the pants with his stick. Young was immediately banished from the game, but afterward he flashed to reporters a devil's grin and cracked, "Aw hell, it's about time I showed that I was human. The way I'd been acting and preaching all the time everybody probably wondered if I'd become a saint."

Young made it back to the NHL with both Detroit and Chicago again, but he eventually slid back to the minors. Since 1969, he has played for Vancouver and Rochester and now plays for the Phoenix Roadrunners in the WHL. Young loves the Phoenix area and hopes to buy a ranch and settle there someday. The fans have made him the most popular hockey player that Phoenix has ever had, and although Young still collects penalties by the fistful, he hasn't come close to killing someone since he quit drinking.

Young's NHL record of 273 penalty minutes in one season appeared safe for years to come; until Young, only one player in the history of the league, Lou Fontinato, with 202 minutes in 1955–56, had ever drawn more than 200 in a single season. That was before a gangly, red-haired son of a Baptist deacon came along and started picking fights with every player that wasn't wearing a Black Hawks' uniform.

In his first year out of Denver University, Keith Magnuson was a long shot to make the National Hockey League, let alone to win a starting spot on the Chicago defense. He did both in a spectacular rookie year in which he helped win the division.

Keith Magnuson studied karate and boxing to better prepare himself for the rigors of NHL competition. "My heart's where it's supposed to be. If it wasn't, they'd have run me right out of the league."

Late that season, Magnuson sat in a Toronto restaurant the night before a big game with the Leafs. The kid's hair was slicked down like a choirboy's, and his tie was puffed just so above the vest of his glen plaid suit. In dress, Magnuson has gone a bit mod since his first year in the big league, but his philosophy on the game is still as open and honest as his Huck Finn looks and Wheaties grin.

"All my life I've wanted to play in the NHL," he said. "From the time I can remember, it's all I've ever wanted to do. My dad insisted that I go to college, but the main reason I did was because Denver was a good hockey school and I'd be able to prepare for a hockey career while getting an education. I mean, we practiced three hours a day and played a thirty-six-game schedule.

"But I knew everybody would be running at me my first year here. In this league the first thing they try to find out is where your heart is. My heart's right here, where it's supposed to be. If it wasn't, they'd have run me right out of the league."

Preparing for the anticipated rough reception, if he could stick with the Hawks, Magnuson spent the summer prior to his rookie year working out and taking lessons at Kumilk Goody's Karate Club in Denver. "They were a mistake—the karate lessons," Magnuson admitted in the Toronto restaurant. "In karate, I was planning to go for the nose, make their eyes water. What I hadn't realized was that in karate the basic weapon is your feet. That doesn't do you much good when you're on skates."

Maggie, as he is called, shook his head disconsolately. "Also, in karate you've got to be able to square off with a guy. But this year they've always seemed to grab me and tie me up. I haven't had much room to maneuver. My arms are always tangled up in my sweater or something. This summer I'm going to take boxing lessons."

He did—10 lessons with Johnny Coulon, a former bantamweight champion. And during the summer of 1970, the apartment that Magnuson shared with teammate Cliff Koroll was transformed into a gymnasium with a speed bag, an exercising bicycle and sparring sessions with Koroll that spattered blood on the walls.

The following year Magnuson led the NHL in penalties for the second time in a row, but this time—averaging almost a fight a game—he broke Young's record with 291 minutes (almost six hours) in the penalty box. "I don't go looking for trouble," Maggie says. "But I get fired up for a game like you can't

Below: The league's fastest fists, Orland Kurtenbach, is also a fine center. *Opposite:* Glen Sather gets Darryl Edestrand to the ice and lands a right.

Top: Jarrett and Fairbairn. *Above
and right:* Bryan Watson. "He's
got a look in his eye like a cat."

believe. On the day of a game just leave me alone. I pick out somebody on the other team to hate. That makes it easier to hate the whole team.

"This is a rough game. You've got to establish yourself as being rough, that you're not afraid. Gordie Howe showed just how tough he was and they left him alone. They respected him. So when they dish it out to me, I dish it right back. If they want to fight, they've got a fight in me. At this very moment I'm doing what I've wanted to do all my life and something like a bloody nose isn't going to worry me. I'll fight anyone, anytime. I've never lost a fight in my life. There may have been a few that I didn't win, but I've never lost one."

For a while during his rookie year, Keith Magnuson felt a touch of awe at playing in the NHL. After all, he was out there with Bobby Hull, Stan Mikita, Howe, Jean Beliveau and all the other stars he had followed as a kid in Saskatoon, Saskatchewan. Back in Saskatoon, Magnuson had mailed away for and received autographed photos from all his favorite stars, including the incomparable Howe, who wrote, "Good luck and best wishes to my friend, Keith. Sincerely, Gordie Howe."

But in Magnuson's first game at Detroit's Olympia Stadium, Howe was less polite. With Magnuson crowding him in front of the Chicago net, Howe dispatched an elbow to the ribs, as if to say, "Lay off, kid." Magnuson promptly shed his gloves and was ready. Howe cuffed the rook's ears and muttered to Doug Jarrett, Magnuson's partner on defense, "He's a tough kid, but he'll learn."

Like Magnuson, Pittsburgh's Bryan Watson has never backed down—which is the big reason the scrappy little defenseman is still in the NHL. Certainly no other player Watson's size (5 feet 10 inches, 170 pounds) has absorbed more punishment while meting it out himself. For a while, when he was with Detroit, Watson shadowed the Golden Jet, Bobby Hull—a Piper Cub covering a B-52. But Watson did the job so well that he scored two goals himself while keeping Bobby off the scoresheet, as the Red Wings eliminated the Hawks in the 1966 play-offs.

His tactics, however, were less than honorable. While the Red Wings insisted that Watson was no dirtier than any other hard-checking forward, the Black Hawks charged that he committed all kinds of infractions against Hull. Indeed, Watson brought out the worst in Hull himself, normally one of the cleanest players in the game. On several occasions Hull ex-

While not known as policemen, players like Steve Cardwell and Glen Sather, armed with sticks and skates, will fight when the occasion arises.

ploded at Watson and found himself goaded into costly penalties.

"He's got a look in his eye like a cat," said Bobby. "He grabs and he holds and he trips. None of the other guys assigned to me pull that stuff. He irritates me. He really does."

After watching Watson cover Hull on television, Terrible Teddy Green remarked, "Bobby just took too much guff from the guy. What he should've done is take the guy's head off the first time they played. Watson wouldn't have bothered him much after that."

For his part, Watson neither confirmed nor denied breaking the rules while shadowing Hull. "I've got a lot of respect for Bobby," he said. "He's a great competitor and a helluva guy. But when I've been given a job to do, I do it."

Such is the spirit that keeps fringe players in the big leagues, and Watson is in his ninth year in the NHL. In 1971–72, he led the league with 212 minutes in penalties. As Toe Blake observed when he was coaching the Canadiens, "Watson has the will to win and that goes a long way in hockey. He spruces up the players on his own team. He doesn't look for fights and he's not really a good fighter. But he doesn't run away.

"Some guys play dirty hockey without getting caught," Blake continued. "There's nothing sneaky about the way Watson hits his opponents. He's just so anxious that sometimes he leaves himself open. Our boys know when Watson is on the ice, and I imagine the same thing goes for the other clubs. You keep your head up and you watch for him."

Sitting in a seafood restaurant in San Francisco one night, Bryan Watson conceded that his face had been donated to the game of hockey. The nose was flat and plastic, the brows gnarled and puffed, and the lids drooped like those on a rubber Halloween mask. The teeth he got after a slap shot in the mouth. The damage has led to a succession of nicknames— "Mumbles," "Blinky, Jr.," "Spotty," "Bolts," "Bugsy," "Wasp" and (courtesy of Bobby Hull) "Superpest." But to Watson, the important thing is that he's still in the NHL.

"Everyone has to make this league in his own way," he said. "Some do it by scoring goals, others by playing great defense, others by stirring things up. A good club has a blend of all these things. I've never had great ability, and I'm not that big for a defenseman. I compensate for it by playing the game as rough as I possibly can."

Taking a page from Watson's book, Pittsburgh became one of the scrappiest clubs in the league—especially after Watson arrived in 1969 when the Penguins were extremely short on talent.

The lack of such an approach has sidetracked more than one hockey team capable of a league championship and Stanley Cup. The New York Rangers are a good example. New York has its hitters in Brad Park, Ted Irvine and Vic Hadfield, and as a club the Rangers may have the slickest passers, skaters and playmakers in the league today. But they have yet to display the killer instinct required for a particular team, a championship or a Cup. The malady was especially apparent in the Rangers' frustrating role as bridesmaid to both the Canadiens and the Bruins in the late sixties and early seventies.

"The Rangers seem to have everything out there," observed John Ferguson. "They're disciplined, they're alert, they're quick. But they're rarely the aggressors. Instead they seem to react instead of act upon the other team. Usually they can win on their superior talent alone, but when they get up against a club like Boston, which is rough and tough in addition to being good, the Rangers' talent isn't enough.

"The only way to beat Boston is to be just as physical as Boston is. To do that you've got to go out there with the idea you're going to kill Boston, not just beat them."

Nobody knows this formula better than the little boss of the Rangers, Emile Francis, who has tried desperately to get roughnecks into his lineup. Players such as Orland Kurtenbach, Reggie Fleming and Wayne Hillman helped bail New York out of the basement in the mid-sixties, but so far Hadfield, Irvine and the like haven't been abrasive enough to induce sufficient respect—or fear—in the opposition. So Brad Park has been going it alone. When he saw the Stanley Cup slipping away as the Rangers fell two goals behind to Boston in the fourth game of the 1972 finals in New York, Park skated up to Bobby Orr and picked a fight. The wrestling match ended with Orr on top, but it was significant that Park was the man who sought to provide the psychological lift that might have turned the series around.

Certainly Francis couldn't be accused of negligence in the search for the elusive quality of intimidation. In February, 1972, it looked as though he might have succeeded at last, when he acquired Jim Dorey from Toronto. The price was high—Pierre Jarry, a promising right winger who had just led the Central

"Everyone has to make this league in his own way. Some do it by scoring goals, others by playing great defense, others by stirring things up."

195

It's almost impossible to keep from fighting in hockey, considering the stimulants: extreme speed, swinging sticks and board checking.

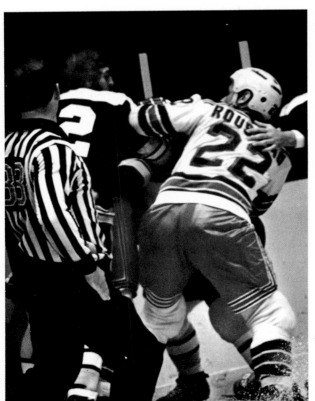

Hockey League in scoring. In Dorey, however, the Rangers got a 24-year-old with a caveman physique and disposition to match, well documented by the 200 minutes in penalties he got in his rookie year. He was also a defenseman with all-star potential.

Dorey had arrived on the NHL scene with the proper awe and respect, but, like Magnuson, he didn't take anything from anyone. He proved it in only his second big-league game, when Ken Schinkel of Pittsburgh flashed past him along the boards. Although the rookie only tapped him on the shoulder pads, Schinkel fell skidding on his stomach. Referee Art Skov, sufficiently impressed, gave Dorey two minutes for tripping. As Schinkel brushed the snow from his uniform, Dorey noticed him grinning. "That was when I realized he'd taken a dive," Dorey recalled. "I went over to him and said, 'You took a dive, didn't you?' 'Sure,' he said. 'What are you going to do about it?'

"That was when I hit him in the mouth."

Before the rookie was through, Schinkel lay face down on the ice again, and Pittsburgh's tough John Arbour was draped semiconscious in the arms of two teammates. Dorey finished the night with four minor penalties, two majors, two misconducts and a game misconduct—a total of 48 minutes and $175 in fines.

"I've got your number," warned Skov.

"Good," quipped Dorey. "Do you want my address too?" (Hence the game misconduct.)

Such was the irreverence Francis was seeking when he reluctantly gave up Jarry. But unfortunately, Dorey dislocated his shoulder while bashing an opponent in his first game with the Rangers and was out for the rest of the season. Then, when the New England Whalers came calling with a fat contract, Dorey jumped to the WHA. Francis was sick.

The "third-man rule," introduced by president Clarence Campbell, has minimized the roughneck contributions a player such as Dorey can make. In an effort to curb the brawling image he felt the game was attaining, Campbell ruled that any player entering a two-man fight would be automatically suspended from the game and fined $100. The rule—good or bad, depending upon to whom one is talking—has definitely stopped the bench-clearing brawls. There have also been fewer fights, since the lesser fighters now realize that once the gloves are dropped, they're probably on their own.

Those fights that do occur now have an honest,

197

clear-cut quality usually absent in overly populated brawls. Now a hockey fight is usually one-on-one, while noncombatants pair off, grab sweaters and glare.

"But the tactics haven't changed," says Ferguson. "The guy who gets in the first punch has the advantage, so if you're going to fight, fight. You're crazy to wait around."

"Flick your glove in his face and pile into him before he knows what's going on," says Magnuson.

Since hockey fights rarely last more than a minute, the man who gets in the first blows rarely comes away with less than a draw. And since balance is essential—but extremely difficult to attain on a slick surface—the man with the short, straight strokes is

apt to land the more-telling blows on the other guy.

To hear the bad guys tell it, the meaner you are, the easier you make it for yourself in the long run. A bloody nose here, a shiner there, a missing tooth or two—or three or more—are all worth the ultimate reward—respect. Certainly Ferguson proved the value of intimidation. When he came up to the Canadiens from Cleveland, Ferguson was a forward of minimum hockey skill; everything about him was average except his competitive instincts and fire. By attacking everybody in sight and quickly establishing himself as a person to be avoided on the ice, Ferguson was free to develop into an excellent two-way hockey player and an integral part of the Canadiens' success. The same was true of Howe, whose hard-earned inde-

"The third-man rule—good or bad—has stopped bench-clearing brawls.
There have been fewer fights because the lesser fighters
now realize that once the gloves are dropped, they're on their own."

pendence allowed him to use his talent to the ultimate. In 25 years, Howe never drew more than 109 penalty minutes in a season, but only because he was a master at retaliating when the referee wasn't looking. Getting too close to Gordie Howe simply wasn't worth it.

After his devastating defeat at the hands of Howe on that February night in 1959, Louie Fontinato was never quite the same. Not only did his face suffer permanent damage, his reputation as a roughneck did, too. Sold to Montreal, Fontinato's career came to an abrupt end one night in 1962 when he crashed into the boards and suffered a broken neck.

The accident probably would have killed anybody else, but in the finest tradition of the bad guys, Louie lived. He retired to the quiet of his farm in Canada— perhaps to ponder what might have happened if *he* had gotten in the first punch against Gordie Howe.

Opposite: At 6 feet 3 inches, Jerry Korab is expected to throw his weight around. It often gets him in trouble. *Left:* Argumentative defenseman Don Awrey.

7 | Twelve Men:
A Consensus Postwar, All-Star Team

GORDIE HOWE

Until Bobby Orr came along, there was little doubt that Gordie Howe was the greatest hockey player who ever lived. Some could shoot harder or skate faster, and some, like Rocket Richard, might have been more opportunistic around the net. But until Orr, no man was ever such a blend of abilities—skating, shooting, scoring, playmaking and the desire to use his strength in personal confrontations. As they used to say, the only thing Howe couldn't do was sit on the bench.

When he finally announced his retirement in an emotional news conference in Detroit on September 9, 1971, Howe had played for more years and in more games than anyone else in NHL history. He had scored more goals, more assists and more points, he had played in more all-star games, had been selected to more All-Star teams and had won more Hart Trophies (most valuable player) and Ross Trophies (scoring) than anyone else.

He scored his first NHL goal in his first game, on October 16, 1946, in Detroit against Toronto's Turk Broda at 13:39 of the second period, with Sid Abel and Adam Brown assisting. His last goal (number 853) and point (number 1,967) came on April 3, 1971, in Detroit against Chicago's Tony Esposito at 1:34 of the third period, with Don Luce and Jim Niekamp assisting. As the Prime Minister of Canada once said, he had truly won the title of "Mr. Hockey."

Howe cruised the rinks of the NHL scoring and setting up goals with the freedom only the ruthless enjoy. "The only way to stop him," says Toronto defenseman Kent Douglas, "is to crowd him, throw him off stride. But nobody even wants to get near Gordie Howe." After a game against the Red Wings, New York's Donnie Marshall was asked what it was like to play against Howe. Marshall calmly lifted his shirt, pointed to a dark-red welt across his ribs and said, "Second period."

"My first game in the NHL was against Detroit," recalls Bryan Watson of the Pittsburgh Penguins. "I was with the Canadiens at the time, and they threw me out to help kill a penalty. I went into the corner with Howe, knocked him down from behind and skated away with the puck. But I hadn't gone very far when I heard this whoosh, whoosh coming up behind me. Then here's this stick slipping up under my arm and the blade not an inch from my nose. It's Howe. 'Check out, junior,' he says."

"When Howe gets knocked down," says another longtime opponent with the Black Hawks, "he looks like he doesn't even care. But as he's getting up, he's looking for the other guy's number. And a little later that guy will have stitches in his head."

For a while, it seemed as if Gordie Howe might play forever. His 1,841 games spanned no less than a quarter-century in the NHL—"a nice round figure," Howe says. States Bobby Hull, "It got to the point where we'd look at the schedule and say, 'Well we've got Montreal on Thursday, Toronto on Saturday and Gordie on Sunday.' "

Still, the magnitude of Howe's 25-year record comes into focus only when it is compared to those with an outside chance to match it. As the leading scorer in hockey today, Phil Esposito of Boston is averaging 1.18 points per game. To catch Howe, he would have to maintain that average for 995 more games—or 13 seasons—at the end of which he would be 42 years old. In goals, Esposito would have to continue his current average of .52 per game for 986 games, or 13 seasons. But perhaps more impressive is the fact that a rookie in the NHL, to catch Howe, would have to average 100 points a year for 18 years and 52.4 goals for 15 years.

Shortly before he died in 1969, Jack Adams, former general manager of the Red Wings, recalled the first time he ever saw Gordie Howe: "It was the first day of our workouts in the fall of 1944, and I had been watching our knowns and unknowns loosen up for a while. We threw some pucks onto the ice, and all of a sudden out of the maze of players comes this big kid who skates in on goal and fires a powerful shot from the right side. Then in the next rush, he lets go another from the left side. I'd seen a lot of kids come and go since I started watching the best pros back in 1916, but this kid was just too much. Both of those shots were good, powerful forehanders; neither had been a backhand hoist.

"I'd seen capable switch-hitters in baseball, but in hockey they're as rare as snowflakes in July. So I called this kid over and asked him his name. 'Gordon Howe, no relation to that other guy,' he says, motioning to Syd Howe, our eventual Hall of Famer, who was also on the ice. 'Well son,' I said, 'if you turn out to be just half as good as Syd Howe, you'll be a mighty fine hockey player.' "

In the fall of 1944, Howe was a tall, gangly youth of 15 with thick brown hair and soft, almost apologetic eyes. As the fourth of nine children of Catharine and Ab Howe, a garage worker, he had been raised in

"Until Bobby Orr came along, there was little doubt that Gordie Howe was the greatest hockey player who ever lived. No man was ever such a blend of abilities—skating, shooting, scoring, playmaking."

Saskatoon, Saskatchewan—and it is doubtful that anyone greener ever became a Red Wing. Perhaps it was because of his youth that the Rangers, who a year earlier had given him a tryout, had released him. "I'll never forget the day he signed with the Wings," said Jack Adams. "He seemed happy enough with the contract—we gave him a four-thousand-dollar bonus—but I found him outside my door with a worried look on his face. I asked him if anything was wrong and he said no, it was just that I hadn't given him the Red Wing jacket I'd promised him when he signed.

"Here was some kid. When he was fifteen he was the best prospect I ever saw, and when he was seventeen he was the best rookie I ever saw. When he was twenty-two he was the best young major leaguer I ever saw, and now, well, everyone knows he's the best hockey player anyone has ever seen."

As Howe was to reminisce after his retirement, "My first ambition was to last a year. In fact, I went around cutting out everything that mentioned me or showed me in a Detroit uniform, just to prove that I'd played in the National Hockey League."

In the NHL, everyone takes a run at the rookies. Howe as a rookie was no exception. On his first road trip, he tangled with Montreal's own legend, Rocket Richard. Challenged in the corner, Howe swung and flattened the Canadiens' star with one punch. "That'll teach you to fool around with our rookies, you phony Frenchman," sneered Sid Abel—and with that, Richard swung and broke Abel's nose in three places.

Howe, it seemed, was always frustrating the Rocket. When Gordie got his hundredth NHL goal in February of 1951, it was in the Forum—on "Maurice Richard Night." And in December of 1958, he got his four hundredth—with Richard checking him. "I saw someone fire from outside, and Howe reached for it," Richard recalls. "I lifted Howe's stick from the ice with my stick, but the puck hit his and went in. I should have gotten an assist on the play."

Until Howe displaced him in 1950–51, Richard had been the first All-Star right wing for six years in succession; after that the two were practically automatic selections at the position for six more years, Howe number one four times and Richard twice, with only Bernie Geoffrion interrupting Howe's dominance in 1953–54.

In late March of 1950, Howe collided with Toronto's Ted Kennedy during a play-off game and suffered a fractured skull, a broken nose, a lacerated

Bobby Hull: "It got to the point where we'd look at the schedule and say, 'Well, we've got Montreal Thursday, Toronto Saturday and Gordie Sunday.'"

right eyeball and severe cuts about the face. He was rushed to the hospital, where he remained in the operating room for three hours while surgeons worked to halt a brain hemorrhage. Howe will shrug and say it wasn't all that bad, but Sid Abel recalls one doctor's having said that when they opened Howe's skull, "the blood geysered to the ceiling." Still, Howe was out of the hospital in time to watch Detroit win the Stanley Cup that spring and went on to lead the NHL in scoring for the next four years in a row.

"He's remarkable under pressure," Jack Adams said. "You always figure when he's on the ice he'll either tie the game or win it. In the dressing room before a big game, he's always just as cool as he is on the ice. No matter what the pressure, he could pass a cup of tea on a stick across to another player and not spill a drop."

From 1947 through 1952, Howe skated at right wing on the famed "Production Line" with Abel and Ted Lindsay, and in 1950, they finished 1–2–3 in league scoring. After coming in second in 1947–48, the Red Wings finished first seven years in a row, second in 1955–56 and first again in 1956–57. During that span the Wings won four Stanley Cups and reached the finals seven times.

On March 22, 1953, with Montreal's Bert Olmstead shadowing him, Howe failed in the last game of the season to score his 50th goal, a feat which would have tied him with the record holder, Richard. Nevertheless, he finished with 49 goals and 46 assists to win his third consecutive scoring championship (and would win his fourth the following year). At the time nobody had won as many as three scoring titles, let alone in consecutive seasons. On April 14, 1955, he scored the winning goal in a 3–1 victory over the Canadiens at Detroit in the seventh game of the Stanley Cup finals. It was the last time Howe would play on a Cup-winning team.

During his career, Howe suffered broken ribs and toes, a broken wrist, three broken noses, damaged knee cartilage, a shoulder dislocation and assorted scalp wounds. But it was arthritis that finally brought him down, at the age of 43. Just before he began his 25th season, Howe had undergone an operation on his arthritic left wrist, but another attack soon flared in his right elbow. Then, during a game in Philadelphia, he fell heavily across a skate and tore cartilage in his rib cage that sidelined him for a month. He began to hint that the end might be in sight. Although nobody was sure at the time, Howe's last game—number 1,841, including play-offs—was a 6–0 loss to the Rangers in Madison Square Garden on April 4, 1971.

"I could have played another year," he said six months later. "But why tear down in one year what I've worked so hard to build in twenty-five? Sure, I needed fourteen more goals to reach eight hundred. But is getting fourteen goals that important? I don't think so. In fact, it's being selfish, and I would have been cheating the Detroit fans, who've been so wonderful to me.

"Actually, I'd been thinking of retiring for the last five years. Then last winter, with all the aches and pains, I began to think about it more and more. When my mother died in June, I asked myself, 'Hey, what are you doing?' One of the last things she said to me before she died was that she hoped I would quit be-

fore I got hurt. I regret deeply that she died without knowing my decision."

Thus one of the most remarkable careers in all of sport came to an end. Obviously, the loss was nowhere felt more than in the red-carpeted dressing room in Olympia Stadium, where no one will ever pull on the number 9 uniform again. It was in that dressing room that defensemen Gary Bergman and the newly acquired Carl Brewer were removing their gear after a game in early 1970. As Brewer was talking to Bergman, Frank Mahovlich—who had scored the winning goal that night—passed by on his way to the shower. "Way to go, big fella," Brewer called, slapping Mahovlich on the buttocks.

"Carl," Bergman said, "you'll have to find another name for Frank. There's only one Big Fella on this club."

Gordie Howe's career spanned 25 years, in which he played 1,841 games and scored 786 goals. He fought off injury until arthritis forced him out.

FRANK MAHOVLICH

For Frank Mahovlich, the problems began in 1958, the year he beat out Bobby Hull for Rookie of the Year in the National Hockey League. From that point on, he couldn't do anything right. In ten and a half years with the Toronto Maple Leafs he would score almost 300 goals, including 48 in one season. He would make the All-Star team six years in a row and, at times, jerk people from their seats with the brilliance of his play. In 1968 he would be traded, a player who had never reached his potential.

"No matter what I did in Toronto, they wanted more," he would say. "I happened to get forty-eight goals one year, so they expected it every year. And they were always around, talking hockey. I couldn't get away from hockey, hockey, hockey. All the time hockey."

Long before he first appeared in the NHL, everyone had heard of Frank Mahovlich. In 1953, practically every scout in the league tried to sign the big, classically proportioned son of a Croatian coal miner. Toronto eventually prevailed, even though Chicago had offered the elder Mahovlich a five-acre fruit farm on the Niagara peninsula. When Mahovlich was Rookie of the Year for the Maple Leafs four years later, no one was surprised; he was *supposed* to be Rookie of the Year. He was Toronto's long-awaited answer to that string of Montreal stars that included Maurice Richard, Boom Boom Geoffrion and Jean Beliveau. After Mahovlich had scored 22 goals in his second season and taken Boston apart in the play-offs, someone nicknamed him "The Big M"—and it stuck.

Next came a run at Richard's record of 50 goals, which fell short by 2. A year later, Chicago owner Jim Norris offered the Leafs $1 million in cold cash for Mahovlich and was turned down.

By then, however, Mahovlich and Punch Imlach, Toronto's coach and general manager, were at odds in a situation that was only going to grow worse. "Hockey is a streetcar named desire," Imlach would say, "and Mahovlich doesn't always catch it." At the same time, the Big M was scoring 33 goals one year and 36 the next—but because it wasn't 48, Toronto fans only became convinced that he wasn't playing up to his potential. Such was the pressure, from both the fans and the coach, that eventually doomed Mahovlich in Toronto. In November of 1964, he had a nervous breakdown; in 1967, he had another. Finally, in March of 1968, he was shipped to Detroit

"With Toronto he would score almost three hundred goals, make the All-Star team six years in a row and jerk people from their seats with his brilliance of play."

in a trade that involved stars Norm Ullman, Garry Unger, Carl Brewer and Paul Henderson.

Mahovlich became a new man. Sid Abel, Detroit's coach and general manager, placed him on the line with Gordie Howe and Alex Delvecchio. They became the highest-scoring line in NHL history. With Howe then, as always, number one in the hearts of the Motor City fans, Mahovlich scored the most anonymous 49 goals ever—and loved every minute of it. "I've never felt better in my life," he said. "They treat me well. I'm playing with two great players, and I don't worry like I used to. When I was traded, it was as if a big weight had been lifted from my shoulders. I still like Toronto, but it's just that I can play better here."

"I think," observed Howe, "that if the fans in Toronto had given M a chance and cheered him instead of booed him, the pressure might not have cooked the guy. Even though Frank looks so big and strong, I've noticed he really doesn't have that much stamina. He gets pretty tired near the end of a shift, and anyone can look bad when he's tired. In Toronto a lot of people probably thought Mahovlich was loafing when he was really just tired."

But less than three years later, following an upheaval in Red Wing management, Mahovlich was on his way to Montreal. "I wouldn't have traded him if I hadn't been offered both quantity and quality," explained Detroit's new general manager Ned Harkness, who had obtained Mickey Redmond, Guy Charron and Bill Collins from the Canadiens.

Once again, Mahovlich made the change in scenery a change for the better. In 38 games, he scored 17 goals and 24 assists and helped lead the Habs into the play-offs, where they upset the regular-season champion Boston Bruins in the semifinals and went on to claim the Stanley Cup. Mahovlich set play-off records with 14 goals and 27 points in 20 games. Goalie Ken Dryden later said that although he was overjoyed to have won the Conn Smythe Trophy (most valuable player in the play-offs), he did not see how anyone could have contributed more than Frank Mahovlich.

"Getting hot in the play-offs helped me as far as the fans were concerned," Mahovlich admits. "But the truth is, I never thought of Montreal as being like Toronto. From the very beginning, people were friendly to me. They made me feel at home. I never thought about the pressure that might have been placed on me, because nobody treated me as if I had

a lot to prove. I was left alone to play my own game."

"When he plays his game, there's not many any better," says Montreal coach Scotty Bowman. "Just talk to the defensemen sometime. They'll tell you that when the Big M is on the move, there's nobody harder to stop."

"The secret," observes Peter Mahovlich, Frank's brother and teammate in Montreal, "is that he's enjoying himself. For the first time in Frank's life, he's having fun playing hockey."

Although Toronto turned down an offer from Chicago of $1 million cash for Mahovlich, they would eventually trade him to where "they treat me well."

JEAN BELIVEAU

On a cold Saturday night in March of 1971, they held "Jean Beliveau Night" in the Montreal Forum. More than 17,000 persons were there, and among the gifts the Canadien immortal received were a plane trip to Paris, Munich and the Caribbean; a bronze medal depicting Beliveau scoring his 500th goal; an enormous silver bowl from the Canadiens and a set of handmade pipes "for all the great stories" he had provided the Montreal chapter of the Professional Hockey Writers Association. But only when several of his former coaches—including Toe Blake and Punch Imlach—carried out a three-by-seven-foot replica of a $156,000 check to the Jean Beliveau Fund did the big Montreal center's eyes soften with tears. By previous arrangement, all monetary contributions for the night were to be channeled into the Beliveau Fund for Canada's Underprivileged Children. As a trio of boys wearing number 4 jerseys skated around the Forum ice, displaying the check to the crowd, Beliveau stepped to the microphone and spoke in both French and English.

"This is the highest and best thing that could happen to any man," he said. "It is the greatest mark of esteem you could have given me . . . I have always wanted to find a way to repay all you people, and the Jean Beliveau Fund will enable me to say thank you to some of those badly in need of help."

If ever there was a knock on Beliveau, it was that he was just too nice to be a hockey player. At 6 feet 3 inches and 205 pounds, he was more than capable of turning most of his opponents into scar tissue. But throughout his 18 years with *Les Canadiens,* he conducted himself with manners better suited to an Emily Post dinner party. Big Jean did not brawl, and he rarely expressed his displeasure over an official's call; instead, he preferred to play the game in the classic manner, with ease and grace and a style that clearly placed victory above personal accomplishment. "I always felt," said David Molson, former owner of the Canadiens, "that if you could combine Maurice Richard's aggressiveness with Jean Beliveau's ability you would have the greatest hockey player in the world. Of course, you can't do that, for Jean Beliveau is a very sensitive human being."

Beliveau led by example, and when the Canadiens named him captain in October of 1961, passing over older members of the club like Boom Boom Geoffrion, Dickie Moore and Tom Johnson, hardly a

voice was heard in protest. Beliveau went on to lead the team with the richest tradition in hockey as it had never been led before. When he retired on June 9, 1971, Beliveau had played in 1,297 games over 18 seasons, scored 586 goals, 809 assists and 1,395 points—second only to Gordie Howe in the last category. Montreal missed the play-offs only once during his career, finished first ten times, second five times and third twice. The Canadiens won 10 Stanley Cups and reached the finals 13 times.

What *Le Gros Bil,* as he was nicknamed, meant to the Canadiens was perhaps best dramatized during the 1967–68 season, when as late as January 7 the team was in last place. The city was cold and glum, its populace humiliated. But then Jean Beliveau returned after being out with torn ligaments in his knee. The Habs took off, winning 12 games in a row and going undefeated in 16 straight. They soared from last place to first, where they remained for the rest of the year, and went on to win the Stanley Cup. During that 16-game streak, Beliveau scored 10 goals and assisted on 17 more. He finished with 31 goals and 37 assists for the season, and in the 1969 semifinal series against Boston, it was he who scored the goal that finished the Bruins in double overtime of the sixth game.

Indeed, when Montreal was losing stars like Richard, Doug Harvey, Moore and Geoffrion, it was Big Jean who kept the club together. It was Big Jean who could fuse the old with the new, the greatness of the past with the promise of the future, and—more through actions than words illustrate that mysterious pride which had always existed on *Les Canadiens.* When Claude Ruel, a former scout, replaced Toe Blake as coach of the Canadiens, someone asked him how he would handle stars like Beliveau. Ruel looked aghast and snapped, "Big Jean, he would never loaf."

No player—not Richard or Geoffrion or Yvan Cournoyer or Guy Lafleur—ever reached the Canadiens with the weight of publicity that rested on Beliveau's shoulders. In Beliveau's case it was fortunate that his talent was as broad as those shoulders, for pressure was always present. When he had two goals, the people wondered why he had not scored three. And yes, when he had scored three, there were those who left the Forum grumbling that he should have scored four.

"There is a lot of tension in this business," Beliveau said. "What a hockey player does is published in every paper in Canada. Everybody has an

"Beliveau preferred to play in the classic manner, with ease and grace and a style that clearly placed victory above personal accomplishment."

215

opinion of what a hockey player should do. This makes tension. So I will know when the time comes to retire. It is hard to retire when you've had a bad season. And it is hard to retire when you are feeling good. So I wait. I think I will know."

The time came in spring, 1971. The Canadiens had just upset the champion Boston Bruins in the semifinals and gone on to defeat the Chicago Black Hawks in seven games for the Stanley Cup. Jean Beliveau was 40 years old. So he retired, to a job in the front office. He would make special appearances and work for the Molson Brewing Corporation and never have another worry in the world. But to those who had seen him play, especially in Montreal, hockey would never be the same. As Punch Imlach, who first coached Beliveau and who, as coach of the Toronto Maple Leafs, later was often victimized by him, once said, "The only thing I don't like about Beliveau is that he's on the other team."

In 1971, Jean Beliveau played his last Stanley Cup
series. It was a great one—he collected 16
assists against Boston, Minnesota and Chicago.

PHIL ESPOSITO

"I'm not a Bobby Hull, a Gordie Howe or a Bobby Orr," says Phil Esposito. "I've never made people rise to their feet with spectacular plays. I just do my job. To tell you the truth, I wouldn't walk across the street to see myself play."

Phil Esposito isn't as unspectacular as that; modern hockey fans thrive on goals, and nobody scores them better than the big center of the Boston Bruins. But Esposito's style *is* more deceptive than overpowering, more pragmatic than inspiring. All he does is put the puck in the net.

Instead of exploding through the defense and knocking goalkeepers over with the force of his shots, Esposito lumbers up the ice with his shoulders hunched and his head bobbing, appearing to shove the puck along instead of to carry it. No, he is not as fast as Hull, as smooth as Howe or as exciting as Orr, but the laboring style, unspectacular as it may seem, contributes greatly to the remarkable scoring records of Phil Esposito.

"Sometimes he just doesn't look that dangerous out there," says one goalkeeper. "He's all arms and legs, and there are times when he looks like he's really fighting the puck. But just the reverse is true. He's usually under control, and he doesn't rush himself. If he has time, he'll give you three or four moves before he shoots. His shot isn't that hard, but it's quick. And its usually someplace hard to get at."

During 1970–71, Esposito lumbered through a scoring year that Hull, Howe and Maurice Richard never dared dream of. Teaming with Orr to lead the Bruins to the regular-season championship, Esposito scored 76 goals to bury Hull's previous record of 58 and added another 76 assists to break the record of 126 points he had set two years earlier. The following year, under pressure to show it hadn't been an accident. Esposito poured in 66 goals and assisted on 67 more for his third over-100-point season.

Esposito's feats have, of course, been greeted with skepticism by some observers, particularly those who remember the preexpansion days, when goals were much harder to come by. With the luxury of having two big linemates (Wayne Cashman and Ken Hodge) to muscle the puck out of the corner and onto his stick, Esposito can concentrate on setting himself up in the slot and pulling the trigger. However, many of those playing both with and against him insist that Esposito is every bit as good as his record suggests.

He has the unique ability, they say, of slowing a game to a "scoring pace," a pace where plays can first be developed, then finished off.

"He's strong and he's got a fantastic reach," says Orr. "His arms are so long he can reach out and grab a pass most others can't. And with such a reach, he can play farther out in the slot, where the defensemen can't come to get him. If they did, they'd leave themselves open back around the net. Where Espy sets up, most teams just can't crowd him the way they'd like to."

"I've been around the National Hockey League since 1950," says Boston coach Tom Johnson. "I've played with or against some of the best centers in the game—Milt Schmidt, Teeder Kennedy, Elmer Lach, Jean Beliveau. Some are already in the Hall of Fame. But I'd have to say that Esposito is the best I've ever seen. He's strong, and he's got such a wide stance you can't knock him off balance. And I've never seen anyone move through traffic any better."

"When he was growing up, I had my doubts that Phil would make it in the NHL," says Esposito's father, Patrick. "He seemed too slow and too weak on his ankles. But everywhere he went, he led the league in scoring."

Unlike the performer who loves the applause of the crowd and constantly comes back for more, Esposito wants goals, goals and more goals. "I just love to put that puck in the net," he admits. "Even when I'm playing with the kids in my hockey school, I love to score goals. I can't help it, I just love it."

The hockey world will never forget the trade that brought Esposito to the Bruins. Although at the time it appeared to be a good trade for both Boston and Chicago, it has since been referred to as Boston's biggest heist since Brinks, or Chicago's biggest mistake since the lamp was kicked over by Mrs. O'Leary's cow. Milt Schmidt, in his first year as general manager of the Bruins, was in the market for some big forwards. He didn't really care who they were; his team was just getting pushed around too much. At the same time, Chicago's Tommy Ivan had designs on young Gilles Marotte, a tough, hard-hitting Boston defenseman who seemed to have a bright future. Esposito was in the doghouse; he had not scored a point as the regular-season-champion Black Hawks had lost out in six games in the Stanley Cup semifinals with Toronto. So on May 15, 1967, Esposito, Hodge and Fred Stanfield went to Boston in exchange for Marotte, center Pit Martin and goalkeeper Jack Norris.

"If he has the time, he'll give you three or four moves before he shoots. His shot isn't that hard, but it's quick. It's someplace that's hard to get at."

Esposito remembers that he was at a banquet in his hometown of Sault Ste. Marie when his wife called with the news. "I was really shook by it," he says. "I knew they hadn't been enchanted with me in Chicago. But I had been seventh in the league in scoring, even though they said I got a lot of 'garbage goals,' or rebounds off shots by Bobby Hull. But more than anything, I think they wanted me to be big and rough and bruise people. That wasn't, my style."

Also, going from a first-place team to one that had won only 17 games the year before, Esposito felt that he would be losing a substantial amount of play-off money. "You won't miss it," Schmidt said. "With you, we're going to make the play-offs."

"Naturally, I couldn't believe him right away," says Esposito. "But a few weeks after training camp opened, I began to get his point. I've always been a positive thinker, maybe even an egotist. And I began thinking I could actually help this team make it."

The rest is history. The Bruins soared. The Black Hawks sagged, but finally recovered from their last-place finish in 1969 by winning four straight division titles. Esposito, an ebullient personality despite his long face and sad eyes, fit into the Bruins' locker-room scene as well as he did on the ice, contributing more than anyone else to the happy-go-lucky spirit which has been the Boston trademark ever since. He has, he admits, found a second home.

"I liked Chicago," he says. "I liked the guys I played with. Bobby Hull is still one of my best friends. But in Chicago Bobby and Stan Mikita were the big guns, the guys who made the big money. Now I've wound up in a similar position here in Boston, and I like it. In fact, I couldn't be happier."

BOBBY HULL

In the spring of 1972, while the World Hockey Association was convincing a number of National Hockey League notables to play for their league, it still felt that in order to make itself respectable it would have to sign one man, the biggest name in hockey, Bobby Hull.

In June of 1972, Hull signed with the WHA's Winnipeg Jets for almost $3 million. It was reported on the front page of the *New York Times*. It was featured in *Time* and *Newsweek* and analyzed in financial sections of many newspapers. In all, hockey in general—and Hull in particular—received miles of print during a month when the only time people usually think of ice is when there isn't any in their glasses.

But then, Bobby Hull isn't just another hockey star. In fact, few athletes have had the impact on any sport that Hull has had on the game of hockey. Throughout the sixties, Hull was indisputably the number-one attraction in the game, a glamorous blond who brought fans to their feet wtih his daring rushes, who sent them home buzzing about his thunderous slap shots. And off the ice, well, there just wasn't anyone else like Bobby.

"To say that Bobby Hull is a great hockey player is to belabor the point," explains his former teammate Stan Mikita, a star in his own right. "He's all that, of course, but what I admire most about him is the way he handles crowds. He really enjoys signing autographs. I only wish I enjoyed it as much as he does. At banquets, he's really quite hard to believe. He talks so casually and charms so many people, I'll bet he could talk in a graveyard and arouse the dead."

When Hull left for Winnipeg in the summer of 1972, it was understandable that the NHL was more than a trifle upset; the established league was losing one of its brightest stars, and where Hull had gone, others were sure to follow. "He's like an evangelist," argued one NHL attorney. "Children follow him and hockey players follow him."

Still, Hull hadn't been the happiest hockey player in the world—and has said so on numerous occasions. He was fed up with the constant fouling by opponents whose sole purpose was to keep him off the scoresheet, and his run-ins with the Chicago Black Hawk management had left scars. He was tired of "big-city phonies" who latched onto him just because he was a hockey player. He longed for the day

Hull was signed by the Black Hawks in the fall of 1957, the youngest player ever signed by Chicago. But it wasn't until 1959 that he began scoring big.

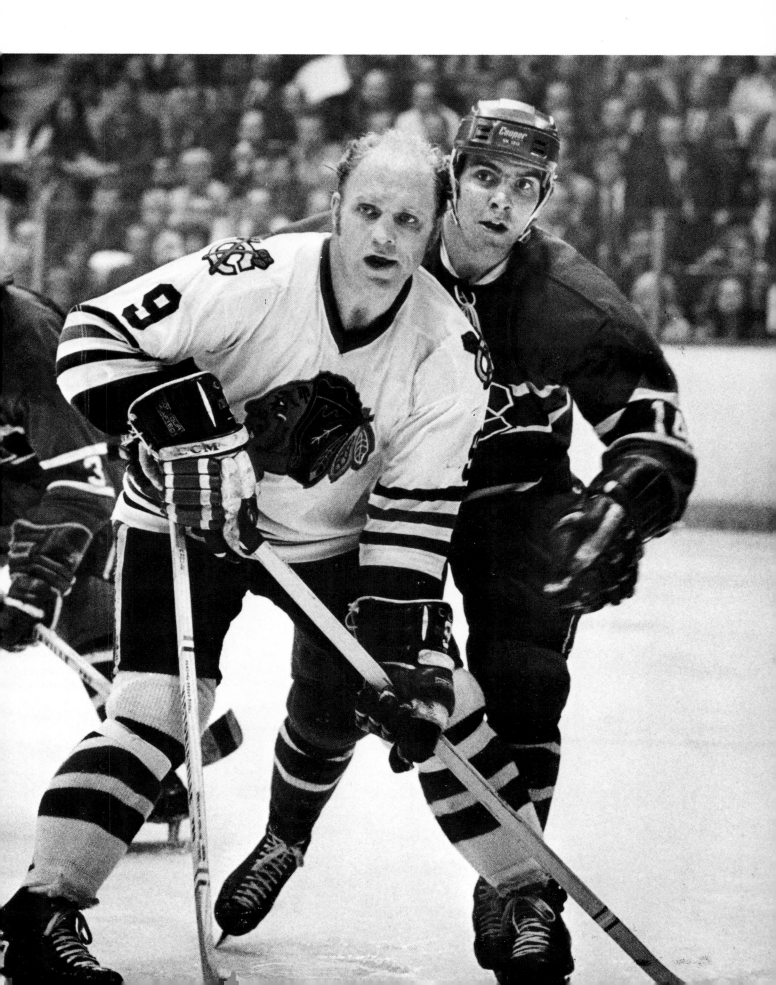

when he could retire to his ranch in Canada and spend the rest of his life raising polled Hereford cattle.

"Bobby's a complex individual," a close friend once said. "There's a lot of the Canadian farm boy in him, but he knows that his game is played in the big cities and that's where his income is. So he's learned to play the sophisticated role, to be the kind of person they expect him to be in New York and Chicago. But I'm not sure he really likes it. I think he'd be perfectly happy staying on that farm back in Ontario."

Records? They seemed to mean little to Hull. Once, after he had scored goal number 681, he was asked if he thought he could break Gordie Howe's record of 786. "Look," Hull replied. "Most of Gordie's goals came the hard way—before expansion. A lot of mine did too, but I would rather have Gordie keep the record than to have someone say the only reason I broke it was that I played more seasons against expansion teams. Besides, records just don't mean that much to me anymore."

Expansion, too, had taken something out of Hull. There had been a great deal of pride associated with playing in a select, six-team league, he said. But that pride was now gone, and with teams being added almost by the year, he doubted that he would ever get it back again.

All this started building to a climax in December of 1971, when rumors circulated that Ben Hatskin had offered Hull $1 million to join his Winnipeg franchise in the new World Hockey Association. In February, Hull was picked by Winnipeg in the league's player draft, and by May he had acknowledged that he had made "a verbal deal" with the club. Still, it wasn't until June 27—when Hull indeed signed with Winnipeg —that anyone really believed Hull would make the switch. But, following gala celebrations in both Minneapolis and Winnipeg, Hull explained that he finally had what he had wanted so much these past few years—lifetime security for his family, a chance to continue his hockey career and live on a farm at the same time.

"I'm a small-town boy at heart," he said. "I think we had more dogs than people back home in Ontario. We made our own fun and learned about the small things in life. Here in Winnipeg, we're going to return to that sort of thing and buy some livestock and about a thousand acres to move around on."

Bobby Hull is a small-town boy. As one of 11 children of Mr. and Mrs. Robert Hull, Sr., he was born in January of 1939 and reared on a farm near Pointe Anne, Ontario. He grew up raising cattle, shoveling snow, pitching hay and mending fences, and it all contributed to his magnificent body. And back then, hockey was Hull's whole life.

"Saturday night was hockey night," he recalls, "and our whole family would gather around the radio to hear Foster Hewitt broadcast the game from Maple Leaf Gardens. Nobody could broadcast the game like Foster Hewitt: 'And here we are, ladies and gentlemen, awaiting the start of the third period between the Chicago Black Hawks and the Toronto Maple Leafs. The score is tied 2–2, and the Leafs will be defending the south goal, the goal to our right. . . .'

"Those games meant so much to us, we'd be out on the ice the next day, pretending we were Maurice Richard and Elmer Lach and Gordie Howe, playing in Maple Leaf Gardens. Once in a while, Mum and Dad would take us to Maple Leaf Gardens. I'll never forget, we'd have to stand in line for what seemed like an eternity, but then we'd finally get tickets, and I'd run ahead, up the stairs to the balcony, where I'd always try to get a place on the railing and hold my arms out to save a place for Mum and Dad.

"And one night, I'll never forget, I waited after the game to get Gordie Howe's autograph. When Gordie came out, I was afraid to walk up to him. But my Dad pushed me and said, 'Go ahead, go ahead, it's all right.' I did, and I'll never forget how much that autograph meant to me. . . ."

Hull was signed by the Black Hawks in the fall of 1957, the youngest player ever given a contract by the club. But he was a center, and during his first two years in the league he scored only 13 and 18 goals, respectively. Then, during the play-offs in the spring of 1959, coach Rudy Pilous switched Hull to left wing, where he promptly became the most feared shooter in the game. Hull led the league with 39 goals in 1959–60, dropped to 31 the following year, then scored 50 in 1961–62 to tie the record shared by Maurice Richard and Bernie Geoffrion. Now whenever he stepped onto the ice—both at home and on the road—the arena would hum like an overloaded cable.

Goaltenders shuddered at the thought of facing his shots, which reached speeds of 120 miles an hour. When Hull adopted the curved stick, his shots not only streaked, they also dipped, sailed and curved. "There were times," recalls retired Toronto goalie Johnny Bower, "when I just couldn't see Bobby's shot. I'd see him wind up, and I'd have an

Although his records didn't mean that much to Hull, they made him the richest player ever when he decided to play for the World Hockey Association.

idea where it was going to go, but I'd lose it anyway. It was just too fast. One of the things I'm thankful for is that I got out of the game before I was hit in the head by one of Hull's shots."

Hull led the league again in 1963–64 with 43 goals. He got 39 in 1964–65, then soared to 54 the following year. Goal number 51, against Cesare Maniago of New York on March 12, 1966, was, at the time, compared to Roger Maris's breaking Babe Ruth's longtime home-run record of 60 in one season. In all, Hull scored 50 or more goals five times during his NHL career, a record in itself, and his personal high was 58 in 1968–69. Not surprisingly, he made the All-Star team 12 of his 14 years in the league, including the last 9 in a row.

In the fall of 1969, Hull had a conflict with the Black Hawk management that has smoldered ever since—Hull claiming at the time that the Hawks were reneging on promises made the previous year, when he signed a four-year contract for $400,000. After missing the first month of the season, Hull returned to score more than 130 goals over the next three years, but things were never the same. As Hull would say later, "Chicago made me an excellent offer, but even aside from the financial security, I'm excited about going to Winnipeg. In a way it's almost like going back home."

"There were times," recalls Johnny Bower, "when I just couldn't see Bobby's shot. I'd see him wind up, but I'd lose it anyway. It was just too fast to see."

MAURICE RICHARD

In all the history of sport, Maurice ("Rocket") Richard is the only athlete ever to have had a riot in his behalf. Inevitably called "the Richard riot," it occurred the night of March 17, 1955, and lasted into the small hours of the morning. There was looting and burning over a 15-block area of downtown Montreal, and when it was over, 37 people had been injured and 70 arrested.

But then, no one in the long and distinguished past of the Montreal Canadiens could arouse the Forum multitudes like the Rocket. In the eyes of the people of French Canada, Richard was not only a hockey hero but also a symbol of the strong, courageous warrior leading the fight against hate and persecution. One glimpse of that Gallic glare and they would follow him anywhere.

An opposite view of Richard was more popular in areas outside Quebec and the Maritimes. Once, in his column for the French newspaper *Le Samedi-Dimanche*, Richard wrote that Leo Labine of the Boston Bruins was ashamed that he could not speak French, his native tongue. Labine answered that, despite his French name, his mother was Irish and his family had lived in English-speaking Ontario for years. But on his next visit to Montreal, Labine came prepared. Having been coached by a teammate, Real Chevrefils, he skated up to Richard and said, *"Comment ça va, mon vieux? Prenez garde ce soir."* Incensed, Richard jabbed back with his stick, to which Labine replied in cold, even English, "Look Rocket, you've got thirty-two teeth. Want to try for sixteen?"

Nevertheless, no one brought fiercer dedication to his trade—and in the Rocket's case, that was hockey and hockey alone. Richard had no outside business interests. After a game, he might have a beer and a cigar, but no more than one of each. There was only one way he knew how to play the game—hard. During one practice session, he and his younger brother Henri collided with such force that both were knocked unconscious. Both were cut, the Rocket worse. Henri woke up first and stood anxiously over his brother as the trainer worked to revive him. Finally the Rocket came to and, looking up, said, "You had better take care of yourself, Henri. You are liable to get hurt."

What Richard did best, of course, was score goals, and the way he did it left Forum crowds in hysterics. A small bull of a man at 5 feet 11 inches and 190 pounds, he played the "off wing"—a left-hand shot on the right side—and appeared to run over the ice instead of to skate on it. Once across the blue line he would dip a shoulder into the defender and cut in on goal with strength amazing for a man his size. "There was just no stopping him," recalls goalie Don Simmons. "When he was bearing down upon you, his eyes shone like headlights on a truck. It was terrifying."

Between 1945 and 1955, Richard led the NHL in goals five times. In the 1944–45 season, he not only became the first player to score 50 goals but did it in only 50 games. His lifetime total of 626 goals is exceeded only by Gordie Howe's and Bobby Hull's. In the clutch, he had no peer; most of those who saw him play still say that, if given the chance to choose a player to win the biggest game of the year, that player would be Rocket Richard. "He just seemed to rise to the occasion," says Red Kelly. "The Rocket was very difficult to keep under control in a money game."

"He was an explosive scorer," says Billy Reay. "He could break up a game faster than anyone I ever saw."

No one ever broke up a game like Richard did in the 1944 Stanley Cup finals against Toronto. Although only 23 years old, he had already won special attention from every team he had played against. In this one—on March 23 in the Forum—his shadow was a husky forward named Bob Davidson. Davidson had one duty—to stay with Richard and let his teammates worry about offense.

The teams skated through a scoreless first period, but at 1:48 of the second, Richard scored to put Montreal on top, 1–0. Seventeen seconds later, he scored again. Toronto drew to within 2–1, but at 16:46, Richard scored his third goal of the period, even though he had spent four minutes in the penalty box. One minute into the third period, he scored his fourth, and seven minutes later, his fifth. The Canadiens won the game, 5–1. They went on to take the Cup in five games, and Richard's five goals remain a record today. "The Leafs always put Davidson on me," Richard recalls. "Sometimes he got so close it made me angry. That night I guess I took it out on him—and the puck."

Richard's play-off record only underlines his reputation as a clutch scorer. Consider these marks, achieved when pressure was at its peak: most overtime goals (6), most game-winning goals (18), most three-goal-or-more games (7), most consecutive

After a game, he might have a beer and a cigar, but no more than one of each. There was only one way he knew how to play the game—hard. They called him "the Rocket."

Called "Lazy Lightning," he once told his coach, "You think I'm kidding, but I love that puck. As long as it's on my stick, I guarantee nothing bad will happen."

233

as Doug Harvey," said Toe Blake. "But I've learned to swallow in silence."

What else was there to do? From 1951 through 1962, Harvey never failed to make the All-Star team. Seven times in eight years he won the James Norris Trophy as the league's outstanding defenseman.

"But," as he admits, "it was a shame how we treated those coaches. I mean, just playing hockey was so much fun that we didn't give any thought to how they felt. I remember one night in Boston. It's the sixth game of the Stanley Cup finals. We're ahead 4–0, and all we have to do is keep skating and we've got the Cup.

"But before you know it, the score's 4–3. There's less than a minute to go, and the Bruins have their goaltender out. I get the puck and start past the Boston bench when one of their players, Leo Boivin, reaches out and grabs me. But I shake him off. I take a shot. It's blocked, but I get the rebound and score. That makes it 5–3 with twenty-eight seconds remaining.

"In the dressing room afterward, during the celebration, I tell Blake that I hadn't realized there had been that much time remaining; if I had I would have skated around the net a few times before sticking it in. He tells me to get away from him before I drive

him crazy. He couldn't even stand to look at me."

Ironically, there was no more intense student of the game and its players than Doug Harvey.

"You come up with things that work for you," he said. "When they stop working for you, you'd better find out why. If you don't, down you go.

"I was called plain lazy, but when you're out on that ice, you discover there are a lot of guys who are awfully good at hooking the puck away from you. If you're skating fast and lose the puck, it's hopeless to try to recover it. But if you're skating in low gear with the puck out ahead of you, there's still a chance of getting it back if somebody takes it off your stick."

In 1961, at the age of 36, Harvey was sold to New York, where he signed as player-coach. The Rangers had not made the play-offs in three years, nor would they for four years after Harvey quit. But they made them in their one year under Doug Harvey.

"That was the worst year of my life," Harvey recalls. "I couldn't even go out for a beer with the boys."

Beer was one thing that Harvey did not treat with nonchalance. The National Hockey League tried to keep him out of the Hall of Fame because of it, but it appeared that they might relent—primarily because, with the exception of Bobby Orr, Doug Harvey was the best defenseman in the history of the NHL.

From 1951 through 1962, Harvey never failed to make the All-Star team. Seven times in eight years he won the James Norris Trophy as the league's best defenseman.

RED KELLY

A few years ago, someone asked defenseman Bryan Watson why the Pittsburgh Penguins, who had never before made the Stanley Cup play-offs, were all at once cruising to a second-place finish in their first year under coach Leonard ("Red") Kelly. "Well," Watson said, "I look at him standing in the middle of the dressing room, and I think, there's a man with high ideals. He doesn't smoke and he rarely drinks. He never swears and hardly ever raises his voice. He uses excellent English. He's intelligent, he's proven himself in the business world. He was even a member of Parliament.

"But at the same time, he was also a hockey player. Not an average hockey player, like me, but a great hockey player. An All-Star. He played on a lot of championship teams, and he helped win a lot of Stanley Cups. That's all the reasons I can think of for now, but give me five minutes and I'll have ten or fifteen more."

Red Kelly always did seem too good to be true; it makes one wonder how a Toronto scout could have looked him in the eye and said, "Kid, you'll never make it in the National Hockey League. You can't skate good enough." Snapped up by the Detroit Red Wings, Kelly stepped into the starting lineup at 19 and, in his first year, helped the team win the Stanley Cup. Before he was through, Kelly had spent twelve and a half years with Detroit and seven and a half with Toronto, won the James Norris Trophy (outstanding defenseman) once and the Lady Byng Trophy (most gentlemanly player) three times and played in more play-off games than anyone else in NHL history —164, or the equivalent of two full seasons. In all, Kelly played on nine first-place teams and eight Cup winners.

"I never said much about it," he remarked after retiring, "but I really wanted the Cup in Toronto in 1967, my last year. It meant I started my career with a Cup and ended it with a Cup."

Kelly started out as a defenseman and finished as a forward, a feat previously unheard of in professional hockey. Traded to Toronto in late 1960, he was switched to center by Punch Imlach, who the following year placed him on a line with Frank Mahovlich. Mahovlich promptly upgraded his goal total from 18 in 1960 to 48 in 1961. Kelly assisted on 50 goals that year and was named the club's most valuable player.

A year later, the Maple Leafs won their first Stanley Cup in 11 years, and Kelly scored a career

Signed by the Detroit Red Wings, Kelly stepped into
the starting lineup at nineteen and, in his first year,
helped the team win the Cup. He played for 20 years.

Kelly played on nine first-place teams and eight Cup winners and was in more play-off games than anyone else in NHL history. He won the Norris once.

high of 22 goals. He also had a career low of six minutes in the penalty box, but teammate Dave Keon, with only two minutes, won the Lady Byng Trophy. Kelly was not a meek hockey player; he was precise, as certain on the ice as he was in his private life. He had decided that "if you lose your temper while the puck's in play, you're only increasing the other side's chances of scoring." Even in his rare moments of fury, a Kelly expletive never exceeded "dang."

"At Detroit one night, Vic Lynn provoked Kelly into a fight," recalls Milt Dunnell, sports editor of the *Toronto Daily Star.* "Red was a young player with the Wings, and after carefully removing his gloves and piling them neatly on the ice, he practically knocked Lynn loose from his eyebrows."

In the late fifties, Kelly antagonized the late Jack Adams for confronting the Detroit general manager with his team's complaints and admitting to a reporter that Adams had urged him to play on a broken ankle. Traded to New York, Kelly quit—until some behind-the-scenes maneuvering resulted in his being sent to the Maple Leafs, for whom he had wanted to play since childhood. The next night, when Punch Imlach sent him over the boards, Kelly received a four-minute standing ovation, the longest in the history of Maple Leaf Gardens.

Kelly enjoyed the switch to center, for he had always been the type who could carry the puck, control the action, deal a pass. Even as a defenseman, he had stirred the crowd when he broke across the blue line, the puck fastened to his stick, his red head high, looking for a man breaking toward the net. If Frank Mahovlich had a knack for finding a seam in the defense, Kelly was equally adept at giving him the puck as he got there.

In 1962, Kelly was not only centering the Leafs' highest-scoring line of all time, but also commuting almost daily between his home and Ottawa, the Canadian capital, as a member of Parliament from Toronto's York West. Once, it was computed that with tourist-class fare then $38 for the 55-minute flight between the two cities, Kelly spent almost $9,000 of his $10,000 governmental income just getting to work. Explaining why he had chosen to run for political office, Kelly says, "It's easy to complain about how badly things are being run, but not so easy to do something about them. I thought I'd see what I could do. Besides, they had told me I didn't have much of a chance to win—and I never go into anything with a losing attitude."

BOBBY ORR

A reporter, hoping to put into perspective the impact of Robert Gordon Orr on the world of professional ice hockey, decided to get the opinion of an expert. He went to the home-team dressing room in Detroit's Olympia Stadium, to the aging, legendary superstar of the Red Wings, Gordie Howe. Howe was asked what he thought were Orr's best moves. Looking up from the stick he was taping, Howe lifted an eyebrow and replied, "Just putting on those *bleeping* skates."

If there is one thing about which hockey players, fans and executives all agree, it is that there isn't anybody like Bobby Orr. He can skate, pass and shoot the puck, set up goals, score goals, keep goals out of the Boston net. He can command a game—do whatever it takes to put the Bruins on top. Bobby Orr can even fill every seat in the Oakland-Alameda County Coliseum Arena, a feat other teams, much less other players, find difficult.

"Orr does things out there that no other player can do, but a lot of people take it for granted," says Tom Johnson, coach of the Bruins and himself a former All-Star defenseman for the Montreal Canadiens. "But he also does the things that excite the newcomer. The rink-long rushes, the hard body checks and that whistling slap shot. He runs things out there. The puck is on his stick half the game. If you're watching your first hockey game—and lots of people are nowadays—all you have to do is watch Orr and you catch on fast."

It is said that only time will tell whether Orr is the finest player ever, a status, until only recently, reserved exclusively for Gordie Howe. But with each passing year, the Orr skeptics diminish. The cherished trophies and awards have become incidental; they are all but conceded to him now.

"The first time I ever saw him play I knew he was going to be a superstar," recalls Emile Francis of the New York Rangers. "But I didn't think it would happen until he was older. At twenty-two? Never."

"It used to be that a defenseman's job was to play defense," says goalie Gump Worsley of the Minnesota North Stars. "It used to be that they didn't care how many points a defenseman scored. But now they not only look at how he plays defense, they want to know how many points he can score from the blue line. You know who we can thank for that."

Orr is the showpiece of the National Hockey League, and his presence influences everything from television to player salaries. With Bobby Orr in hockey as with Joe Namath in football, nothing has been the same since he arrived.

Amazingly, the Bruins stumbled onto him by accident. Bobby was 12 years old and playing in a pee-wee game in Gananoque, Ontario, 300 miles southeast of his hometown of Parry Sound, when Wren Blair, then director of player personnel for the Bruins, arrived to scout two prospects, Eaton and Higgins. After watching a young kid with a shaved head run the game, Blair immediately persuaded the Bruins to donate $1,000 to the hockey program in Parry Sound. He also set about getting to know Mr. and Mrs. Doug Orr.

Montreal, Chicago and Toronto were already interested, and until Orr signed a Junior A contract, he was fair game. So, when Orr was only 14, the Bruins gave him a tryout. He was so impressive that Blair wanted to sign him on the spot. But Mrs. Orr was not anxious to see her son leave home. Only when Blair proposed that he live at home and commute to and from games in Oshawa, 150 miles to the south, did she permit her son to sign. For $2,800—money enough to stucco the family house, purchase a secondhand car and leave some cash over for Mr. Orr—Bobby Orr signed a Junior A contract with Boston on Labor Day, 1962.

Playing for Oshawa that year, against players five and six years older, Orr made the second All-Star team. The next three years he made the first All-Star team and continually set new scoring records for a defenseman. When he was 16 years old (and all of 5 feet 9 and 166 pounds), Orr was on the cover of Canada's national magazine, *Maclean's*. "Bobby Orr," said the accompanying story, "is a swift, powerful skater with instant acceleration, instinctive anticipation, a quick, accurate shot, remarkable composure, an unrelenting ambition, a solemn dedication, humility, modesty, and a fondness for his parents and his brothers and sisters that often turns his eyes moist."

Orr turned pro early one September morning in 1966, when he signed a contract for about $40,000 (a bonus and two years' salary) aboard the yacht of Bruins' GM Happ Emms in Barrie, Ontario.

Heralded as the player who would lead the Bruins out of the NHL basement, Orr wasn't fazed by the messianic notices. After winning the Rookie of the Year award, he led the Bruins to third place his sophomore year. Boston finished second in 1969 and in '70. In 1971, they won their first Stanley Cup in

"He can skate, pass and shoot the puck, set up goals, score goals, keep goals out of the Boston net. He can do whatever it takes to put the Bruins on top."

29 years—with Orr scoring the winning goal in overtime. There followed two first-place finishes, and another Stanley Cup championship in 1972, during which Orr won his second Conn Smythe Trophy as the most valuable player in the play-offs. By that time he had a lock on the James Norris Trophy, annually awarded to the NHL's outstanding defenseman. He had won three straight Hart trophies (as the most valuable player during the season) and one Art Ross (scoring) award. All at once the Bruins were the power of the NHL. Although players such as Phil Esposito, Ken Hodge and John Bucyk contributed greatly to the renewal, Orr was indisputably the driving force.

It was never better demonstrated than early in the 1972–73 season. Following Boston's Stanley Cup victory over the Rangers, Orr underwent surgery on his knee. He spent the summer in rehabilitation and was unable to compete in the emotion-packed Canada-Russia series in September. Then the NHL season started, and without Orr, the Bruins quickly sank to sixth place. They were still struggling when Orr returned in mid-November in a game against the New York Islanders. Only minutes were gone when Orr scored, on his first shot. The Bruins won that game and their fortunes brightened. Bobby was back, and the Bruins were again back in the fight for first place.

When asked to comment on his feats, Orr is as communicative as Ronald Ziegler. If the Bruins have won by 5–1, and Orr is asked to comment on his two goals and three assists, he will steer the conversation to the Boston goaltender who lost his shutout in the first period. If the Bruins have won 5–3, Orr will ignore his two goals and three assists and defer to the teammate who scored into the empty net, because until then the game could have gone either way.

"Let 'em say all those nice things about me," Orr once said. "I know I make mistakes, and I make plenty of them. They say practice makes perfect, but they're wrong. Practice will make you better, but nothing will make you perfect. At least I'll never be. I do dumb things. Once I was rushing against the Rangers and I crossed their blue line when I heard a voice say, 'Drop it! Drop it!' So I made this drop pass and skated in to screen the goalie, and by the time I turned around, Vic Hadfield was on a breakaway for New York, and he scored. He was the one who was saying, 'Drop it!'

"Every time I start to get a swelled head, I think about that play, or all the other mistakes I've made and still make. If the fans don't notice, well, so much the better."

By everyone else's standards, Orr isn't making many mistakes. Orr is without doubt the most dominant player in hockey since Howe.

"You can't compare Howe with Orr," says Jacques Plante, who, in 20 years, has faced them all. "When one is a forward and the other is a defenseman, it's altogether different. Bobby Orr is trailing the play, and he never has to rush up unless he wants to. He can pick his spots. He can wait until the end of a shift. The players have been on the ice for two minutes while he's been laying back, and all of a sudden the other team is pressing. Orr gets the puck and just leaves those guys behind him because they are too tired to catch up. He could beat them anyway, almost anytime he wanted to, but he has that great advantage of being able to pick his spots. He is very smart out there.

"You watch him at the end of the period with maybe twenty seconds to go. He will rush right up to the opponent's net, right to the goaltender, because he knows that even if they regain the puck, they won't have enough time to attack again. He watches the clock, and then he goes. He can do everything. He's unbelievable."

Says Orr's coach Tom Johnson, "If you're watching your first hockey game—and lots of people are nowadays—all you have to do is watch Orr, and you catch on fast."

PIERRE PILOTE

Pierre Pilote started out tough and ended up cute. But his appearance never changed. The Detroit Red Wings' Ted Lindsay wasn't far off when, during a collision along the boards one night, he told Pilote that his face looked like the Indian head on the front of the Chicago Black Hawks' jerseys.

Growing up in the French-Canadian section of Kenogami, Quebec, Pilote fought almost every week with one of the sons of the English-speaking executives and technical people employed at the town's paper mill. Pierre Pilote's father was a laborer at the plant and a former amateur boxer, known in the area as Paul "Kayo" Pilote. Father schooled son thoroughly in the art of fighting.

"The first English words I ever learned," recalls Pierre Pilote, "were, 'Do you want to fight?' I averaged a fight a week and won my share. I had that animal instinct, you might say."

Although he was a scrawny 5 feet 9 and 165 pounds, Pilote carried such inclinations into hockey. When the Black Hawks assigned him to Buffalo in the American Hockey League, Pilote again averaged a fight a week. He took on everyone regardless of size. Pilote drew 85 penalty minutes in his first year, 108 in his second and 120 in the third. "All I knew was fighting," he recalls. "I thought I had to fight to stay in hockey."

By his own admission, Pierre Pilote wasn't much of a prospect when he arrived in Buffalo. He couldn't skate, he couldn't fake, he couldn't even backcheck. All he could do was fight. "I was a mess," he said.

"Nobody could predict a future for Pierre at the time because he was shy on both ability and size," says Tommy Ivan, general manager of the Black Hawks. "He couldn't move that well and he was really quite small for a defenseman."

Between brawls for Buffalo, Pilote somehow taught himself the rudiments of defense. He was called up by the Black Hawks for 20 games at the end of the 1955–56 season. When he came back the following year, he stuck. Arriving in the NHL at a time when a defenseman's heavy body checking had become less important than his ability to move the puck out of his zone and form an attack, Pilote became a "cute" defenseman. He could poke check the puck from an opponent instead of slamming him into the boards. Best of all, he anticipated the play, taking a wide-angle view of the situation and exploiting it.

Pierre Pilote, 2, in action against the Bruins in Boston. "The first English words I ever learned," he states convincingly, "were 'Do you want to fight?' "

"It takes five years for your head to catch up with your legs," he explains. "I learned most of my style from studying Doug Harvey of the Canadiens. I got to know Harvey's moves so well I could anticipate them. I'll bet I intercepted more of his passes than anyone else in the league."

Pilote quarterbacked the Black Hawks as Harvey did the Canadiens. Stationed at the right point on the blue line, Pilote was the master of ceremonies of the Chicago power play, presenting the puck to gunners Hull, Mikita and Kenny Wharram. Or he would keep it himself, with always one more move in reserve, the puck fastened to his stick.

Pilote's knack for making the right play shows in the statistics. He was always among Chicago's leaders in assists, and in 1964–65, finished eighth in the NHL in scoring—at the time, remarkable for a defenseman—with 14 goals and 45 assists. Pilote won the James Norris Trophy as the league's outstanding defenseman in three consecutive years (1963–1965), and missed the All-Star team only once between 1960 and 1968.

Still, he found time to apply his father's teachings, leading the league in penalty minutes with 165 in 1960–61 and coming close in 1964–65. Once, he distinguished himself by beating up both Richards at the same time.

"Henri had given it to me with his stick," Pilote recalls, "and I had to teach him a little respect. But once I'd started, the Rocket came along and had to try to play big brother. I had no choice but to work him over too."

JACQUES PLANTE

In his career as a goalkeeper in the National Hockey League, Joseph Omer Jacques Plante has never been a favorite of the coaches, general managers and owners for whom he has played. At least, that was so until he reached Toronto, where he is presently alive and kicking them out as well as ever at the age of 43. Plante had displayed a knack for getting under the skin of those around him—and he had always been more popular with the fans than with his teammates. Jacques, it was said, looked out for Jacques first and others rarely. In varying degrees, this attitude led to Plante's departure from Montreal in 1963 and St. Louis in 1970—even though both clubs had enjoyed remarkable success with him in the nets.

During the 1969 play-off finals between Montreal and St. Louis, the Canadiens obviously relished getting a crack at Jacques. "When I see his eyes peering out from behind that mask, my shots, I want them to come from cannons," admits Yvan Cournoyer. "Jacques talks and he talks and he talks," says Jacques Laperriere. "All he does is talk."

Even the diplomatic Jean Beliveau, when asked once why he took an extra moment to stuff an easy shot behind Plante, acknowledged, "Oh, I just wanted to make him swim a little."

Nevertheless, all agree that Jacques Plante is one of the top two or three goalkeepers ever to play the game. Plante may talk a lot, but his record speaks for itself. From his rookie year with the Canadiens in 1953–54 through 1962–63, after which he was traded to New York, Plante won the Vezina Trophy six times, including a record five years in a row (1956–60). In 1962, he became only the second goalkeeper in history to be voted the NHL's most valuable player. While he was in the nets, the Canadiens finished first six times, second three times and won five Stanley Cups, reaching the finals a total of seven times. Plante has had the lowest goals-against average in the league nine times in his career, and four times he has led in shutouts.

Plante was an innovator, who changed the face of hockey more than once. As a teen-ager, he had played for a team whose defensemen had such difficulty skating and passing the puck that Plante had to do much of the clearing himself. Ultimately, he brought his roaming style to the NHL. Although criticized for it at the time, "Jake the Snake," as he was

During his career Plante won the Vezina Trophy six times, including five years in a row. In 1962, he became the second goaltender to be voted most valuable player.

nicknamed, demonstrated the style so effectively that all goaltenders roam to a certain degree today—if only to go behind the net and intercept passes wheeled around the boards.

But Plante is most noted for perfecting the goalie's mask, which was one day to save his life. After suffering two bad facial injuries in practice—a broken right cheekbone in 1954 and a fractured nose and left cheekbone a year later—Plante began wearing a welder's mask during workouts. After another shot was drilled off his forehead in the 1958 play-offs, he and a Montreal businessman set about designing a mask. Plante wanted to wear the mask the following season, but coach Toe Blake talked him out of it. "If you have a bad start, the fans will blame the mask."

Then, during a game in New York on November 1, 1959, a shot by the Rangers' Andy Bathgate slammed into the left side of Plante's face. When he reached the dressing room, the goalie marched directly to the mirror, saying, "I want to see just how bad this is." Seven stitches were required to close a three-inch gash from the side of his nose to his upper lip, and when Plante returned to the bench, Blake said that he could wear the mask if he wanted to. "Good," Plante replied, "because I'm not going back out there without it."

Several months later, when a questioner wanted to know if the mask meant he was afraid, Plante said, "If I jump out of a plane without a parachute, does that make me brave?" Today only one NHL goalkeeper—Minnesota's Gump Worsley—still refuses to wear a mask.

Off the ice, Plante is as subject to nervous tension as any other goalkeeper. He has a constant lean, hungry look, and his cheeks are hollow and drawn. His hair has been flecked with gray for years. Still, he combats the tension successfully with myriad outside interests, from oil painting and soft stereo music to tennis, skiing and Ping-Pong. Plante also knits with professional skill, providing himself with the underwear he uses beneath his pads and uniform. "I was a severe asthmatic when I was young," he explains. "As a result I was confined to the house. And as the eldest of eleven children, I had to change diapers, clean house, sew, knit and cook for the entire family."

Plante's two worst seasons in the NHL were with the Rangers, to whom he was traded in 1963. For the only times in his career, Plante's goals-against average exceeded 2.80 (3.38 in 1963–64 and 3.37 the following year). They were also the only seasons his club failed to make the play-offs. In the summer of 1965, he announced his retirement. "My wife was ill," he says. "Her weight had dropped to ninety-eight pounds, and her blood pressure to eighty-five. She needed me the full year around."

Nobody ever expected to see Plante in the nets again, but during league meetings in Montreal in 1968, St. Louis coach and general manager Scotty Bowman noticed Plante hanging around the press room. After learning that Plante had been working out and was interested in returning to the NHL, he got permission from New York's Emile Francis to negotiate with the goalkeeper. A day later, guffaws filled the room when Bowman drafted the 39-year-old Plante—but it was the Blues who had the last laugh. That year, Plante played in 37 games, led the league with a 1.96 goals-against average and shared the Vezina Trophy with Glenn Hall as the Blues won the division title and reached the Stanley Cup finals for the second straight season. A better goaltending team never played in the NHL. The following season, Plante and Hall again backstopped St. Louis into first place and the play-off finals.

During the 1970 play-off finals against Boston, a searing slap shot was deflected into Plante's masked face, knocking him unconscious. Plante was carried from the ice on a stretcher and treated for a concussion in the hospital. "That mask saved his life," Dr. J. G. Probstein said later. "The puck had struck Jacques right between the eyes, and the mask was shattered on the inside. He couldn't have survived a shot of such force without protection."

As it turned out, Plante would never again appear before the adoring St. Louis crowd in a Blues uniform. In May of 1970, he was mysteriously traded to Toronto for "future considerations." Though the Blues' management never said so publicly, it had felt that the flamboyant Plante had had an unsettling effect on the team.

But in Toronto, Plante never performed better. His 1.88 average for 40 games in 1970–71 was the second best of his career, and his relations with those around him had never been more cordial. As Frank Selke, Sr., former general manager of the Montreal Canadiens, once said, "Most of our French-Canadian players are the shy, retiring type. But Jacques is just the reverse. He has changed goalkeeping for the better."

Plante was innovative. He was the first goalie to roam
from the net and the first to use a mask—both tactics
now unquestionably accepted by most NHL net minders.

TERRY SAWCHUCK

Terry Sawchuck had persistent companions throughout his 20-year career as a goaltender in the National Hockey League—glory, injury, controversy and, finally, tragedy.

Injury plagued Terry Sawchuck all his life. As a boy of 12, he suffered a broken right arm and a dislocated elbow during a backyard football game in Winnipeg. He didn't tell his parents about it; they had warned him against football. Later, the bone chips moved and broke a blood vessel in his elbow, and Sawchuck underwent three operations, during which 60 pieces of bone were removed from the arm. He never could knot his tie after that.

On his 18th birthday, during a game in Houston, an opponent's stick sliced the goaltender's eyeball. Only the purely coincidental presence of a nearby hospital with a specialist saved his sight.

During his career, Terry Sawchuck had more than 400 stitches taken in his face. He suffered seven broken ribs. He lost a number of teeth. His nose was broken twice. He dislocated his left shoulder. His left instep was broken, as was his right hand and its five fingers. He needed more than 175 stitches to repair severed arteries, nerves, tendons, blood vessels and muscles after his left hand was sliced by a skate blade.

In the irreverent view of columnist Jim Murray, "It's not 'til he takes his clothes off that you realize Terrance Gordon Sawchuck isn't a unified man, he's a collection of fragments. He wasn't born, he was zippered. He looks like a statue that was shattered, and put back together in the dark."

There is no telling how good Sawchuck might have been had he not been plagued by injury. Even so, he is surely one of the top two or three goaltenders in the history of the game. Like his injuries, Sawchuck's records speak for themselves.

Terry Sawchuck played in more games (971) than any other goalie. He was the first player to win the Rookie of the Year award in three different leagues (Central, American and NHL). His record of 103 career shutouts seems unbreakable. He won the Vezina Trophy three times, shared it once, and five times finished the season with his goals-against average below 1.99. In 1952, when the Detroit Red Wings won the Stanley Cup in four-game sweeps of Toronto and Montreal, Sawchuck turned in four shutouts and allowed only five goals in the eight games.

Like an artist, Sawchuck was a moody and unpre-

In 1956, Sawchuck announced that his nerves were shot.
"I've quit and I'm gonna stay quit," he declared.
He continued to play hockey for 14 more years.

Sawchuck played in more games than any other goalie,
was the first player to win Rookie of the Year
in three leagues and has a record 103 career shutouts.

dictable loner. Traded to the lowly Boston Bruins in 1955, Sawchuck told owner Walter Brown in the midst of his second season that he was finished with hockey, that his nerves were shot. "I've quit and I'm gonna stay quit," he declared.

Detroit general manager Jack Adams had other ideas. He talked Sawchuck back into the Red Wing nets, where he remained until 1964, when Sid Abel (who had replaced Adams) failed to protect the 34-year-old goaltender in the draft. Toronto's Punch Imlach grabbed him. "I knew his record," Imlach said. "His age didn't matter. I told him to throw his birth certificate in the garbage can."

"It was a gamble that I lost," Abel admitted later. "I didn't want to lose Terry."

In Toronto, Sawchuck teamed with another old head, Johnny Bower, to give the Maple Leafs the goaltending that led to the Stanley Cup. During the 1967 semifinals against the powerful Chicago Black Hawks, Sawchuck achieved what many still insist is the finest single exhibition of goaltending in play-off history.

The Black Hawks, who had won the league title on the scoring of Bobby Hull and Stan Mikita, were heavily favored to win the Cup. The series was knotted at two wins apiece when the teams took the ice at Chicago Stadium for the fifth game. With Bower in goal for the Leafs, the Hawks swarmed in on net for the first 16 minutes of the game. They led only 1–0 near the end of the period, but Imlach called Bower to the bench.

"I asked him how he felt," Imlach recalled. "He had missed one I thought he should have had. Johnny said that his hand was giving him trouble, so I asked Terry if he wanted to go in."

Sawchuck entered at the start of the second period. Suddenly, alone with the puck to Sawchuck's left was Bobby Hull. He fired. Sawchuck fell. For a moment, it appeared the goaltender had been struck in the head. Actually, the puck had slammed into Sawchuck's shoulder, where an ugly black bruise showed after the game. "They say the best way to handle Hull's shots is to get out of the way," Sawchuck said. "But I didn't."

Sawchuck got in the way of almost every shot. Attacking in waves, Chicago outshot Toronto by 49 to 31, but the Leafs won, 4–2. Sawchuck was the difference from which the Hawks never recovered. The Leafs eliminated them in the next game and then won the Stanley Cup in six games against Montreal.

"Never have I seen such goaling," said Bobby Hull.

"I have," said Marcel Pronovost, a Leaf who had played with Sawchuck in Detroit. "That guy's been putting money in my pocket for years."

Things were never the same for Terry Sawchuck. Allowed to protect only one goaltender in the league's original expansion draft that June, Imlach kept Bower ("I had to; he'd been with me longer."), and Sawchuck was snapped up eagerly by the Los Angeles Kings. He was not the public relations attraction the Kings had anticipated, however, nor was he the goaltender he had once been. Sawchuck was traded to Detroit, and then to the New York Rangers. In April, 1970, he and his roommate, Ron Stewart, were scuffling on the patio of their apartment house on Long Island when Sawchuck fell backward over the barbecue and suffered a ruptured spleen. A month later, he died during an operation on the injury. Hockey had lost perhaps its finest goaltender.

"It's not 'til he takes his clothes off that you realize that Terrance Gordon Sawchuck isn't a unified man, he's a collection of fragments. He wasn't born, he was zippered."

Acknowledgments

A book such as this one evolves, and in my case this took place over a number of years and through countless conversations with hockey players, coaches and executives who, as a rule, enjoy nothing more than an opportunity to talk about their game. Nevertheless, there are those without whose cooperation and/or indulgence, much of this book would not have been possible. These people are as follows: Ron Andrews, John Ashley, Wren Blair, Red Burnett, Clarence Campbell, Bill Cook, Wally Cross, Joe Crozier, Mrs. Joan Foster Dames, Ken Dryden, Red Fisher, Cliff Fletcher, Emile Francis, Bill Friday, John Halligan, Ned Harkness, Wally Harris, Bruce Hood, Punch Imlach, Tommy Ivan, Norm Jewison, Cesare Maniago, Scotty Morrison, Jacques Plante, Sam Pollock, Don Ruck, Bill Torrey, Frank Udvari and Gump Worsley.

But inasmuch as the actual writing was up to me, there are three persons to whom I owe special thanks for their constant encouragement, consideration and faith in this project. They are my wife Chris and my mother and father.

Gary Ronberg
Chesterfield, Missouri
January, 1973

All photos by **Melchior DiGiacomo** except the following:
Michael Albanese: 14, 102, 146–47, 190
David Bier: 213, 216–17, 229, 230, 231, 249
Peter Mecca: 86, 113 bottom, 162, 163, 169 bottom, 241
Richard Raphael: 21 right, 65 bottom left, 73 bottom, 85, 96 bottom
Ken Regan: 205, 206, 207
United Press International: 210, 211, 212, 216, 220, 221, 226, 233, 236–37, 238, 239, 244, 245, 250, 252, 254, 255
Eddie Wagner, Jr.: 116–17
Wide World Photos: 224, 234, 246